RUSSIAN LETTERS OF SPIRITUAL DIRECTION
1834–1860

RUSSIAN LETTERS OF SPIRITUAL DIRECTION 1834-1860

MACARIUS
STARETS OF OPTINO

Selection, Translation, and Foreword by
IULIA DE BEAUSOBRE

ST VLADIMIR'S SEMINARY PRESS

Library of Congress Cataloging-In-Publication Data

Makarii, Monk, 1788-1860
    Russian letters of spiritual direction, 1834-1860.

    Translation of the author's letters selected from the 1880 ed. published by Lavrov, Moscow, under title : Sobranie pisem blazhennyia pamiati optinskago startsa.

    Reprint of the 1944 ed. published by Dacre Press, Westminster.

    1. Christian life—Orthodox Eastern authors.   I. Title
BX382.M34213   1975   248'.48'19   75-1064

ISBN 0-913836-23-0

Originally published in March 1944
by DACRE PRESS, Westminster

Contents

Foreword

The starets Macarius of Optino was a spiritual director of lay people, monks, and priests. *Starets*—a synonym of *starik,* the Russian for "old man"—implies all the veneration given to an "elder," but none of the conventional respect which surrounds him. The call to be a starets comes late, after a long life devoted to the cultivation of simplicity and humility. The way—for himself and for his disciples— lies through obedience and prayer, and it exacts a constantly deepening love of God and of all creatures. In the words of Igor Smolitsch,[1] the great warm heart of a starets revives the shrunken, frozen hearts of those who flock to him; his perfected will reforms and sustains the imperfect wills of those who place themselves under his guidance.

The tradition of the startsy (plural for starets) goes back to the Desert: to those hermits who were sought out in the solitudes of Egypt, Palestine, or Syria by men eager to find a teacher capable of bringing order into their confusion; capable of kindling the light of hope in the darkness of their despair.

It is tempting, and may be helpful, to elicit the subtle relation of disciple and starets by drawing analogies between the disciple and the Arthurian knight: The monk—or future monk—plods on foot, or jogs on his donkey, through harsh, rugged wasteland; the knight rides forth on his charger in quest of the Holy Grail. Both face dangers, imaginary and real: griffins, basilisks, lions and bears; dragons, unicorns, wolves and boar. Both gladly brave

---

[1]Igor Smolitsch, *Leben und Lehre der Starzen,* Wien, 1937, p. 29.

disaster on the way to the light. But the Celt is intent on contemplating light captured in an intangible cup; the man of the Mediterranean, on learning about the light from another man, and on seeing the light stream forth from that man; indeed, on conversing with it.

At first the men of light were seldom priests, none deeming it important that they should be; but years of rigorous monastic discipline, and of pondering on the Scriptures, were considered essential. These practices, sanctified by grace, made a starets. When he was become, a rumor spread, and disciples gathered.

By the fourth century, the term πνευματικὸς πατὴρ is well established in patristic writings.[2] And it seems that in the first centuries novices and monks travelled far to seek guidance of a "spiritual father," and to make their confessions to him.

As the attraction of desert hermitages decreased, lausiac communities and, afterwards, mountain monasteries gained importance; and one starets after another settled in the vicinity of the new foundations. By the eighth century a confessor is not infrequently attached to a monastery. In time this becomes the rule, and when a starets lives within reasonable distance it is mostly he who hears the confessions.

In the meantime the practice and teaching of the startsy (whose aim is theosis: deification, divinization) had also undergone a change. An elaborate form of the Jesus Prayer—the prayer of the publican—was included in their discipline, henceforth rooted in humility, obedience, silence, recollection, and the Jesus Prayer. (The mental Jesus Prayer varies from a simple recitation, in moments of perplexity or danger, to a system which affects even the body

---

[2]"Pater spiritualis" in *Verba Seniorum,* Migne, *Patrologia Latina* 73, 833-1066.

through the breath and heartbeat; only the simple Jesus Prayer can be safely used without guidance.)

It was at Mount Sinai, in the leading community of early eastern monasticism, that the elaborate Jesus Prayer evolved. By the seventh century the practice had become a tradition among the Sinaitic contemplatives. Mount Athos, which matured to leadership in the eighth century, incorporated the tradition of Sinai within its own, and in the fifteenth century passed it on to Russia.

There may well have been startsy in Russia at any time after her Christianization in the tenth century: the Orthodox east is a homogeneous whole and has a common spiritual climate as well as a common tradition; Russians think of Anthony of Kiev (*d.* 1073) and Theodosius (*d.* 1074, *can.* 1108) as early Russian startsy; but Nilus of Sora (1453-1508) is the first Russian starets to be recorded and generally recognized as such. He spent several years at Athos and devoted much time to study of the eastern masters of contemplation: Anthony, Ephraim the Syrian, Pseudo-Macarius of Egypt, Isaac the Syrian, John Climacus, Abbot Dorotheus, Maximus the Confessor, Simeon the New Theologian, Nilus of Sinai, Gregory of Sinai, and others. Soon after his return to Russia, Nilus fell out with Joseph of Volokolam (*d.* 1515), the Metropolitan Daniel (*d.* 1547), and the monk Philotheus, originators of the expression "Moscow the Third Rome" and propagators of the policy it implies. Outwitted in politics, Nilus retired into solitude on the banks of the Sora, thence to reform Russian monasticism. Because he and Joseph disagreed upon the question whether monasteries should possess lands and serfs, he is known as the leader of the Non-Possessors, a political party. But he was also the founder of Russian "skete life," life in the Russian Scete. Disciples who gathered round him lived the contemplative life, each one by himself or sometimes two together, in shanties that they put up at a considerable distance the one from the other

9

in the great Russian forest. They assembled only for church services, and relived in northern forest land—boggy in summer, frozen stiff in winter—the rigors of the Desert Life.

The Nilus tradition, lying low in its "dark forest," survived the physical and spiritual upheavals that Russia entered upon in the sixteenth century. The loss to the Church, in the seventeenth century, of the large body of dissenters later called Old Believers, caused men to face spiritual problems with renewed courage; the church reforms of Peter the Great (early in the eighteenth century) reawakened in the masses a desire for direct and unofficial spiritual guidance: Tsar Peter had subjugated church life to the Synod, a department of state.

Events and policies combined to create a demand. The response, given by the starets Paissy Velichkovsky, came in the second half of the eighteenth century; this response reaffirmed the Nilus tradition and blended with it.

Paissy (1722-1794), born in Poltava, came of a family of "hereditary" Orthodox priests; but his mother was the granddaughter of Mandia, a devout Jew. Paissy, become a novice, set out to find a starets willing to instruct him. For years he wandered through the eastern Ukraine (the country of his birth), and Moldavia (the Promised Land of many Russian monks in those years when tsardom hampered monasticism in Russia, and the Turks crushed Orthodoxy in Greece). He was professed at Medvediev, but could still find no starets and in 1746 at last arrived at Athos, to settle there. In spite of his spiritual loneliness his reputation for insight and learning grew and, eventually, others begged him to give guidance to them. In 1758, at the age of thirty-six, he consented to be ordained, giving in to the insistent prayers of his disciples and to the reiterated advice of the older monks.

After he and his fifteen disciples had put up the sixteen huts of the new Skete of St. Elijah, it became more generally known that he founded his instruction on the Jesus Prayer and on a detailed, profound knowledge of Scripture and the Fathers. He had become a leader.

But life did not run smoothly. The practice of the Jesus Prayer was attacked by some, others accused Paissy himself of heretical interpretations of Holy Writ. At last in 1763 hardships, occasioned by the Turkish fiscal system, induced him and his fifty monks to leave Athos and settle in the Dragomirna, on the frontier between Moldavia and the Bukovina. The new foundation adopted the rule of Athos. Paissy devoted his days to the economic and spiritual life of the monastery, and reserved his nights for literary work: the comparing of Greek and Slavonic texts, and the retranslating of such as were too inaccurate to be worth correcting. One of his monks was at the same time translating the Fathers into Moldavian.

Paissy had started comparing and correcting texts while still at Athos; his insistence on a deeper and fuller understanding of the Scriptures and the Fathers led him to it. But manuscripts in Greek were difficult to come by; most of these he acquired only a short time before he left, and his more important translations were undertaken later.

Translations, however, were not his only contribution to Eastern Christian thought during his Dragomirna years. In 1763 he wrote a book in six chapters on the Jesus Prayer (a detailed and careful apologia of the practice), and in 1766 a long letter to the priest Demetrius (an important exposition of the rule of poverty, obedience and love, which was followed at St. Elijah's and at Dragomirna).

To the distress of Paissy and his monks, their quiet, studious life soon came to an end: from 1766 to 1778 Moldavia was the battlefield of Russia, Turkey, and Austria; Paissy at once opened the monastery gates to the wounded, and to women and children seeking refuge.

The war over, Austria exacted from Turkey a piece of territory which included Dragomirna. Paissy and his 350 monks, fearing life under Austrian rule at a time when Uniate contentions were bitter, accepted the hospitality offered them by the Abbot of Sekoul, another Moldavian monastery.

But their sojourn at Sekoul was even shorter: Paissy arrived there in the autumn of 1775 and, almost at once, resolved to organize a school of translators; many studious monks gathered round him living four, five, and six in one cell. When the Gospodar of Moldavia, Prince Muruzi, heard of this enthusiasm and of these conditions, he respectfully insisted on Paissy and most of his monks moving to the great monastery of Neamt, founded in the fourteenth century. Paissy, after hesitating for a while, consented to do so in June 1779.

The Neamt school of translators and copyists quickly gained the reputation it deserved. Former translations from Greek into local tongues were amateurish, haphazard and inaccurate. Paissy now trained his monks to compare texts in several languages. He also insisted on their inserting marginal notes which explained the translator's reason for his choice of one rendering, and included most of the rejected ones.

Another important innovation introduced by him at Neamt was the frequent reading of the Gospels and the singing of hymns in Greek, Slavonic, Moldavian, and Russian, during church services.

Soon his reputation for learning and sanctity reached even the Turks, who often allowed men hurrying to and from Neamt to pass on their way without showing their permits, or answering the usual questions.

In Russia interest in the school was considerable, and many Russian novices and monks went there; returning to their own country they imparted to their monasteries Paissy's admiration for the rule of Athos, his devotion to the tradition of the Desert, his ideals and ideas.

Paissy Velichkovsky's translation of Isaac the Syrian

12

into Slavonic is regarded as his most important literary work; it was completed in 1787. But his lifelong fight for the recognition of the Jesus Prayer, waged against such monks of Athos, Moldavia, and Russia as spurned it, is of equal importance.

In 1781 war once again broke out. Austrians and Turks swept over Moldavia, advancing and retreating in turns, until the Russians, led by Potemkin, occupied Jassy. In 1790, Ambrose (Archbishop of Poltava, attached to Potemkin's suite) visited Neamt, gave his official approval to the bond already established between Russian monasticism and the Moldavian monastery, and conferred on Paissy the dignity of archimandrite.

Paissy died on November 15, 1794, aged 72, and almost blind. He is revered in the Orthodox East as a judicious regenerator of monasticism and a conscientious writer and translator; and he is loved as a starets, as one who had acquired the art of consoling and guiding men and had tried to pass on his wisdom to others. His mark on modern Russian Orthodoxy is important, although his adult life was spent beyond the border: his scholarly rendering of the old books, in which he sought information and found inspiration, incited even the laity to think theologically; his Russian disciples, who soon acquired lay spiritual children, showed to these the way of applying to their own lives the Neamt tradition, handed down from the earliest days of the Desert and enriched by Sinai and Athos.

During Paissy's lifetime his influence remained diffused through the whole of Russia. But soon after his death it gathered in the monastery of Optino, in central Russia, near the town of Kozelsk in the province of Kaluga. In 1800, the monk Theophanes—a Cossack pupil of Paissy, and passionate propagator of the teacher's ideals—settled there. When several other admirers of Paissy joined Theophanes, one of these, Abraham, was appointed abbot by Plato, Metropolitan of Moscow. (In the Neamt library there is a book of sermons of the Pseudo-Macarius, sent to Paissy by Plato; it has an inscription dated 1791.)

Theophanes died in 1819, but in 1821 Philaret, Bishop of Kaluga—another admirer of Paissy—founded the Optino Desert (*Pustyn* or *Skete*), and in 1829 the starets Leonid came there. Leonid, instructed in the Paissy tradition by a disciple of Paissy's who lived in another Russian monastery, opens the line of Optino startsy whose popularity was equal among lay people and ascetics.

Macarius, second of the great startsy of Optino, arrived at the skete in 1834 and, after Leonid's death in 1841, became leader of Paissy's Russian following. This position he retained until his own death in 1860.

Optino, monastery and skete, was still inhabited before the war [World War II], though the monks were no longer there. The railroad takes you from Moscow to the town of Kozelsk; the rest of the way—about four miles—you walk, unless you can negotiate with a peasant going in the same direction a lift in his cart.

Almost at once the cobbled street changes into a dusty cross-country road which winds through cultivated fields of barley, wheat, and rye. On the left, the view is limited by smooth rolling hills, on the right, by forest. Far ahead, in the northwest, hills and forest meet at an acute angle, or seem to.

After a while the road turns to the right; the white monastery is before you. Pressed against the somber green of the fathomless forest, it thrusts a bunch of large and small onion-domed turrets into the sky. In days of opulence, the onions were bright gold; later, in days of parsimony and persecution, they turned a mild blue.

At midday in summer, when the abundance of light blurs outlines, the golden cross that tops every blue cupola seems suspended in the sky. The reflection of the glittering host of hovering crosses is usually the first thing that draws the newcomer's attention to a sheet of water spread out at

14

the foot of the monastery. Then he sees the whole building reflected in a stretch of river so still and lying so low that its unobtrusiveness seems intentional: an effect loved and often created by the builders of Russian monasteries.

The cart, after skirting the bank, trundles across a rickety wooden bridge. During the spring and autumn floods, the river unites with lakes, streams and marshes into a huge expanse of water. But in summer there is only a trickle under the bridge; to the left, a stream lazily flows toward distant fields: a sluggish stream hidden by weeping willows that bathe in it their roots and sweep its face with their dripping branches, it is known as Ophelia's Backwater to the educated inhabitants of the neighborhood. Further to the left, a keen-eyed observer may catch sight of another bend of the Zhizdra river with wide sandy banks, flat, whitish, and splotched with patches of dock, as tall as a man.

The cart turns into the forest. Underfoot dry pine-needles lie, inches thick. The girth of some of the trees is so great that four men can hardly join hands round them. Straight and branchless the trees rise, tapering gently. The color of the trunks, a warm mauve above the roots, gradually changes to flesh pink about half way up. If you look still higher you see at last the distant dark green branches, tranquil or blown about, against the sky. Birds sing on all sides. You may even hear a stork clap its beak, in its high-perched nest.

The cart comes out on to a clearing, pulls up before a long high wall, whitewashed and protected from the weather by a diminutive roof of blue-green tiles. Massive wooden doors, studded with nails, are placed in the middle of the wall which rises to form a squat belfry over them. An icon, built in over the doors, has a sanctuary lamp firmly fixed under it. There was a time when the lamp burned night and day. And even now a discrete hand will light it when winter blizzards grow dangerous to tree, horse and man.

Inside the doors the small pink church of St. John blocks the view. Looking right and left you realize that the wall is quadrangular and encloses a large orchard with small houses dotted about, some whitewashed, others built of unpainted wood. Outside the walls, the pines tower so high above the enclosed fruit trees that the skete rests, as it were, in a deep hollow, protected from the winds which blow over fields and hills. Walk round the pink church, and you will see a fishpond glinting at the far end of the enclosure. There are masses of flower beds everywhere, and a good kitchen garden in the left front corner.

In this orchard-skete Macarius spent the last twenty-six years of his life. His whitewashed hut stands about a hundred paces northwest of the church, and consists of three whitewashed cells with an anteroom each. The entrance is a small wooden porch painted the same dark red as the roof-slates, but the wood is almost hidden with vine.

The cell Macarius lived in has two small windows, one looking south, the other east; its large, low stove, like a huge chest, is built of brick and faced with tiles. The room smells of dried apples and incense.

Look out of the east window towards St. John's and if you know where to look between the trees of apple, pear, and plum, you can glimpse Macarius's grave by the west wall of the church. He rests between Leonid, the starets who preceded, and Ambrose, the starets who followed him.

The names of three more startsy are known: Anatolius, Joseph, and Nectarius, after whom names were no longer put on record.

Macarius (Ivanov), priest-monk and monk of the full habit, born in 1788, was a little man with an ugly face, and with a stammer which did not prevent him from conversing at length on intricate subjects. A good musician, he played the violin when a boy, and later became an expert in church music. Of a mild disposition, he loved flowers and books. His family, who owned property in the province of Orel, belonged to the landed gentry. When a young man Macarius thought of marrying, but, in 1810, on a visit to the "Desert" of Ploshchansk, he was so impressed by the monks' saintliness and by the beauty of the church services that he did not return home, deciding on the spot to become a novice.

From the outset he was fortunate in his director, Athanasius (Zakharov), who, a disciple of Paissy, had great influence with monks, church dignitaries, and laymen. For twenty-four years Macarius lived at Ploshchansk under the guidance of Athanasius, and it was the death of his starets that caused him to begin a correspondence with Leonid. The great friendship which ensued led to his leaving Ploshchansk for Optino where, for seven years, he helped the aged Leonid in his work of guidance. The two startsy consulted on most matters and even wrote letters together.

A comparison of Leonid, Macarius, and Ambrose—the three first startsy of Optino—may serve to elicit the startsy's way of blending tradition with freedom. Their sayings passed on by word of mouth, the legendary episodes of their lives treasured in the villages round Kozelsk, and their letters of direction, testify to the tradition they followed and to the freedom they enjoyed.

Leonid (Nagolkin, 1768-1841), a merchant's son, big and strong, had the quick wits usually ascribed to men of his father's calling. Outside the monasteries his influence was greatest with peasants and small townsfolk. A good speaker, he delighted in witty repartee and coined succinct phrases without stopping to think. Occasionally he affected the simplicity of the village fool, always to great purpose.

Macarius, the gentle scholar, was the director chiefly of educated men and women. His rambling letters abound

17

in quotations and learned allusions; they are long-winded and rather dull, but the verbosity is often pierced by rays of remarkably lucid thought and flashes of astonishing insight.

Ambrose (Grenkov, 1812-1891), son of a church reader, was private tutor and schoolmaster before entering Optino at the age of twenty-seven. Both Leonid and Macarius were his directors and contributed to his spiritual growth. A strange mixture, Ambrose was a quick-witted contemplative endowed with profound insight into temporal affairs and into character. Tall, broad in the shoulders and narrow in the hips, he looked like the average Russian peasant. But his eyes shone with unusual directness, and, while he was still young, his long, thick beard turned a patriarchal white. Gay and lively despite ill health, and possessed of a sharp mind and a golden heart, he was loved by many and respected by all: statesmen sought his advice on matters of national importance, and peasant women turned to him when their geese and turkey chicks were dying of an epidemic.

The advice which these three men give is almost invariably a concrete answer to a particular situation, and they insist on its not being thought of as a generalization or used as a general rule of conduct for all. They convey the certitude that taken out of its context their advice is no longer true to their tradition; but that it is true to the tradition when kept in its context; indeed, that it enriches the tradition, and that such additions—of unprecedented solutions for new situations—prevent the old tradition from ossifying.

The startsy do not generalize. They aim at a synthesis, and seek to encompass within their living tradition all human problems. Whoever does such work must needs do it in his own way: not that he interprets the tradition in his own individual manner but, applying the generally accepted interpretation to a unique case, he gives to it the coloring of his own personality. This coloring he is free to give, indeed cannot avoid giving; but this freedom requires of him humility, courage and tact, if his guidance is to remain true to the spirit of the tradition.

The startsy hope—as those who seek their guidance assume—that, when at last the Kingdom does come out of the timeless into time, the entire life of the Orthodox will have been gathered up into the stream of this tradition which is a discipline, a world outlook, and the way of man's conscious collaboration with the will of God.

A comparison of the letters of direction of the three first startsy of Optino—contemporaries and striking personalities—shows the manner in which Eastern spiritual directors blend personal originality with their tradition; even the letters of Macarius alone offer some indication of it.

A great letter writer, Macarius corresponded easily, at length, and with many people. But his letters, to monks and laics, are not the only writings he has left. Imbued with the Neamt ideas he gathered round him monks and laymen, capable of helping him to translate into Russian the life and works of Paissy Velichkovsky; the life and some of the works of Simeon the New Theologian; the works of Nilus of Sora, Isaac the Syrian, and Barsanuphius; some of the works of Theodore of Studios, Abbot Thalassius, Abbot Dorotheus, Mark the Ascetic, Isaac of Egypt, Maximus the Confessor, and other patristic authors.

The work of publishing did not cease at Optino after the death of Macarius. Built by him on a solid basis, it was continued by Ambrose and others.

The original from which the present selection is made, is the second edition of Macarius's *Letters to Lay People,* published by the Optino Skete, and printed in Moscow, by Lavrov, in 1880.

There are 447 letters, some extremely long. They cover practically the whole of the starets period of his life, the earliest being dated September 11, 1837, O.S. (about three years after he settled in the Skete) and the latest, March 19, 1860, O.S. (a few months before his death in September).

There is nothing to show that the second edition differs from the first. The same preface and the same epigraphs (a text out of the Gospels and a quotation out of a sixteenth-century letter) are used in both. In their short preface the editors do not disclose their names or supply any information about themselves, but they give two lists which may be of interest.

They first trace the descent of Macarius as a writer of letters of direction; it opens with three Fathers (Isidore of Pelusium, Nilus of Sinai, and Jerome) and, curiously enough, goes straight on to Paissy Velichkovsky, Theophanes of Novozero, Philaret of Glinsk, Philaret (priest-monk of St. Savior's, Moscow), George the Hermit, and Macarius of Optino.

The second list consists of books referred to by Macarius in his letters. They are: the Old and New Testament; the *Philocalia*,[3] Moscow, folio and quarto (the years

---

[3]Compendium of extracts on prayer and recollection, chosen from the works of the Eastern Fathers; first published in Greek, in Venice, 1782. Nicodemus (1748-1809, sometimes called the Hagiorite), monk of one of the Greek monasteries on Mount Athos, was the chief initiator and editor of this work. Paissy Velichkovsky's translation of the *Philocalia* into Church Slavonic—first published in Moscow in 1793—is called *Dobrotoliubie,* which title has been kept in the Russian translation. The *Dobrotoliubie,* less complete than the *Philocalia,* begins with Anthony the Great (fourth century) and ends with Gregory Palamas (fourteenth century). Peter Damascene, included in the fifth volume of the *Philocalia,* is omitted in the *Dobrotoliubie;* his writings were separately translated and published, in two volumes, by Optino, in 1874. The title *Philocalia* is used in this selection for the Greek, Church Slavonic, and Russian editions. [Selections from the *Philocalia* have been translated into English by E. Kadloubovsky

of publication are not indicated); *Lenten Sermons of Isaac the Syrian,* Neamt, 1812; *Seven Sermons of the Venerable Macarius of Egypt* (ed. not indicated). Also the following works edited, published, and in some cases translated, by Optino: *Life and Works of the Moldavian Starets Paissy Velichkovsky,* 1st ed. 1847, 2nd ed. 1848; *Gleanings for Spiritual Refreshment,* translations from the Fathers by Paissy Velichkovsky, 1849; Nilus of Sora, *Conferences on Monastic Life,* 1849; Barsanuphius and John, *Introduction to the Spiritual Life,* 1851; Simeon the New Theologian, *Twelve Sermons,* 1852; Isaac the Syrian, *Spiritual-Ascetic Sermons,* 1854; Abbot Thalassius, *Chapters on Love, Continence, and Spiritual Life,* 1855; Abbot Dorotheus, *Instructions and Letters,* 1856; Mark the Ascetic, *Moral-Ascetic Sermons,* 1858; *The Ladder of St. John Climacus,* in several translations into Church Slavonic and Russian.

Two points are stressed by the editors in the Russian preface: all names of people and places, and all references which might serve as a clue to the identity of Macarius's correspondents, are deleted. The carefully explained motives were no doubt reasonable at the time of publication, but after a hundred years the scruples, and the meticulous pruning which ensued, seem regrettable.

The second point, the decision to preserve unchanged the style of the letters, is gratifying: Macarius was no master of style, but his medley of styles—involved and clear, wordy and precise, high-sounding and trite, slangy and sublime—is so expressive that it produces a mental

and G. E. H. Palmer, *Early Fathers from the Philokalia,* London, Faber and Faber, 1954; and *Writings from the Philokalia on the Prayer of the Heart,* London, Faber and Faber, 1951. *The Ladder of Divine Ascent* of St. John Climacus, to which Macarius often refers and of which excerpts are included in the second volume of *Dobrotoliubie,* also has been translated into English, by Archimandrite Lazarus Moore, London, Faber and Faber, 1959.]

portrait of him, invaluable where no painted one can be obtained.

The arrangement of the English letters has, however, been chiefly influenced by the Russian editors' lack of method, of which they were, apparently, unconscious. In the original the letters are, on the whole, arranged chronologically, and each letter is given a serial number; and there is no classification. From No. 1 to No. 447 the letters follow each other without a break; but the general chronological order is interrupted when a letter starts a series addressed to one person, and such series follow their own, speeded-up, chronological order. This alone would be confusing enough: Macarius wrote to some of his "children" from his first years in Optino to his last days; but the confusion is increased through some letters being placed at random, both in the general and in the speeded-up chronologies, and others not being dated at all.

As there seemed to be no advantage or reason in retaining the order of the original, an entirely new arrangement had to be adopted; and the English letters are gathered into eight groups under the Beatitudes. This conforms with the Russians' ideal of a Christian life and expresses the aim of the startsy. Yet it was not premeditated. The selected passages seemed to gather under these headings out of an inner necessity; and since "Each one of the Beatitudes asserts that there is a spiritual world which is out true home,"[4] the grouping under the Beatitudes has been retained.

An endeavor has been made to preserve the peculiarities of Macarius's style as far as English permits. Where possible, all selections from one letter have been kept together, but they are separated by ellipsis when the different para-

---

[4]Russell Maltby, *Christ and His Cross,* quoted from *Report on the Proceedings at the Church Unity Octave* p. 48.

graphs are irrelevant to each other, or if a considerable amount of the Russian text has been omitted. The number placed at the end of a passage is the serial number of the Russian letter.

Where Macarius's references to the *Philocalia* are not clear, these have been replaced by references, in the notes, to the 4th Russian ed., St. Petersburg, 1904.

I want to thank Fr. Lev Gillet for reading the foreword in manuscript, the Reverend Patrick Thompson for his suggestions about the arrangement of the letters, and Dr. Nicholas Zernov for generously putting at my disposal his library and his extensive knowledge.

IULIA DE BEAUSOBRE

Teaching them to observe all things whatsoever I have commanded you.   *Matt. 27:20.*

Do not ask counsel on such matters of me, a poor and miserable monk: neither insight into the heights of heaven do I possess, nor the ability to plumb the bed of the seas; neither the gift to measure the ends of the world, nor the learning to check that measure; neither the cleverness to throw causeways across swift rivers, nor that of building firm banks to open lakes; neither understanding of the regulation of the universe, nor the knack to circumscribe it by the thin circle; neither the intention to reduce all human kind to one temper, nor the ambition to thrust evil—and the scheming of evildoers—out of the world; neither this, that, nor the other knowledge or ability is given to me; to me, a wild and senseless sinner, and no doer of good. Only the word of God and the writings of the Fathers can I proclaim to those who burn to listen and pant to accept: to those who thirst for salvation.

Anonymous letter of a Russian monk, 16th century

I

Blessed are the poor in spirit: for theirs is the kingdom of Heaven

1. Direction

What I write to you, I write for you alone, and I must ask you to refrain from passing any of it on to others as a general rule of conduct for all. It is nothing of the kind. My advice to you is fashioned according to your inner and outer circumstances. Hence, it can be right only for you. [108]

Yes! There can be no doubt that under these circumstances a man requires special help from God, and the guidance of a wise man experienced in the fight. [94]

It is certainly a great consolation, and a great help on the way, to find a director under whose wise guidance our will is cured of self-will, our mind of self-regard. But in these days, it is most difficult to find one. [92]

I am afraid you have written to me only because you have illusions about me. You tell me almost nothing about yourself: you say nothing about your social background, family life, obligations, or connections. But how can I, thus kept in the dark, hope to form a right judgment on the particular situation on which you consult me? I am, indeed, hard put to it to find a particle of firm ground on which to build my reasoning. I fear you have not realized that, being unworthy of the grace of seership, I cannot have recourse to supernatural means of knowledge. Still, I shall endeavor to do my best for you. [78]

You say that I have helped your aunt. That cannot be. Only the mistakes are mine. All good advice is the advice of the Spirit of God; His advice, that I happen to have heard rightly and to have passed on without distorting it. . . .

I shall try to answer you as best I can, but you must pray. Pray that God may grant me the ability to say the right words which will bring you help. Pray too, that He may grant you the right faith: faith in our Lord as the lord of all wisdom. No good can come of this letter without His special help. [124]

It was with shame and consternation that I read that passage of your letter where you ascribe to me qualities and virtues in which I know myself to be sadly lacking. May the Lord reward you according to your faith: may He help me really to become such as you think I am. [258]

It is difficult for me, uneducated and insignificant as I am, to give advice to you who have been guided, for many years, by one of our most eminent churchmen. My mind is poor; my heart is even poorer! But being loath to augment your sorrow by a refusal, and placing all my hope in our Lord's guidance, I shall try:

Above all follow carefully every instruction of the great counsellor and friend who has left us.[1] And—since he insisted that you should—refrain from attempting the

[1]In the Russian text there is evidence that the deceased was a bishop, although his name and his diocese have been deleted.

monastic life, but remain where you are, alone in your peaceful retreat.

And since he instructed you in the rule of silence, keep to this as rigorously as he would expect; I mean, in the measure and manner he indicated.

Then you will certainly have to limit the number of people you see. The scruples you elaborate—hurting their feelings and so on—are not important enough for you to break, because of them, the obedience you still owe him. [120]

I cannot possibly give her any guidance unless she herself asks for it. And even if she did, I am doubtful whether I could: her mind is divided, she is quite uncertain as to what it is she wants; and at times she doubts if she wants anything at all.

I can only answer direct, sincere, and simple questions put with simple faith. God Himself sees to it that such questions receive the right answer. An insincere question, put halfheartedly, is no question at all. Confronted by it, I can get no help. I should not know how to answer it. As to your playing the piano, that has nothing to do with your spiritual life and I have nothing to say on the matter. [103]

I do not like the way you have of repeatedly exclaiming that after I have read this letter of yours I shall be disgusted with you. Nor do I like these assurances that it cost you much and that you are smarting with shame. I think, by now, you yourself will clearly have seen from what source all this uneasiness and anxiety spring.

In truth I am, of course, profoundly touched by your frankness: it shows your affection for me. And this only augments my compassion for you, making me even more anxious to find for you the right counsel. If you had joyously described your successes on the path, I, examining my heart, could have found nothing to say in answer.

May the Lord increase your wisdom, strengthen you on your thorny way, and bless you, your husband, and your children. [232]

I am very much to blame for having offended you with my unwise letter. You are right, I was indeed at my wits' end, torn between visitors, my work, and my immense correspondence. Besides, I was feeling so ill, so weak, that I could not find in my empty and shallow mind suitable answers to all the problems that came pouring in.

But you must not conclude that I had rather you did not describe your difficulties to me. Tell me all about them; but pray that the Lord may grant me the wisdom to find the right words for your consolation and guidance. And, in order to make things a little easier, perhaps you could underline the *questions,* thus singling them out from the rest of the text? [249]

As to this life insurance, since I have read nothing on the matter in the Scriptures or the Fathers, I can say nothing about it. Knowing nothing at all about such matters I can neither permit nor forbid your taking this step. Nor can I give you my blessing for it, or even offer advice. But read Matt. 6:34. [252]

Since these thoughts bring into your inner life such embarrassment and commotion, they must have been suggested to you by the devil. The right thought brings with it certitude, courage, and peace. Strive for that.

As to those who are happy without seeking spiritual direction and quite blissful without bothering much about the deeper Christian life—the life of the mind and heart— theirs is the peace of this world, not the peace of our Master.

Whenever we set out firmly to tread the inner path, a

storm of temptations and persecutions always assails us. It is because of this dark host that spiritual direction is profitable, nay necessary, to us whether we retire to a monastery or continue to live in the world.

But those who blissfully ignore the deeper issues and implications of Christianity, and are quite happy without bothering much about anything, know nothing of the peace we seek and of which we drink now a drop, now a draught, all along our stormy, harsh, and bitter way. [245]

How can you say that your spiritual sores can be cured by none but me? Who am I? Dust and ashes, cast in the likeness of the unregenerated Old Adam.

Seek help of our merciful Lord Jesus Christ whose loving wounded heart is open to all. His pure blood is always there to wash away our sins. Keep near the great physician. Seek Him, call Him, knock at the door.

He came down to call to Him sinners, not the righteous and the good. Whenever you have sinned—and no matter what your sin be—run to Him and do penance, firmly resolved to refrain in future from sinning in this way.

If my advice and instruction have ever helped you, praised be the Lord! Realize, however, that it is not really I who have done this but the Lord's mercy, which is granted you according to your faith. [312]

I have told you nothing that is an invention of my own. All of what I say comes from the writings of the Fathers.[2] Mine is only the humble work of choosing passages suitable to your particular case.

And this humble work has been of the greatest profit to me, since it has freshened up much that was growing dim in my constantly weakening memory. So you must

---

[2]Eastern and Russian Fathers mentioned in the Foreword.

see that there is no occasion at all for you to thank me so extravagantly: *Not unto us, O Lord, not unto us, but unto Thy Name give the praise (Ps. 115:1).* May we all constantly sustain each other by counsel and through prayer. [213]

2. Self-Knowledge

Do not limit yourself to striving for the right outward order: fasting and prayer. Strive also for greater inward order, only to be attained through intensified love and deep humility.

You say that the longing for obedience has pierced your heart, and you ask, "How can I attain to it?" Shall I tell you?

In the world you live in, Princess, you must have seen how long it takes an artist to train for his art, and how much effort he must devote to it. Is it not natural that the art of arts should exact even more time and even greater effort?

Pray that you may be granted the grace to read the Fathers with the right understanding, the grace to live up to the standards they put before you, and the grace clearly to see your own frailty. You will not long be left wanting and waiting. God will give you help.

In the meanwhile carefully examine the movements of your heart, the pattern of your thoughts, the intention of all your words and actions. In your case, it may even be good to do this in writing. It may help to make more clear to you your utter poverty; it may humble your pride of mind. [102]

It is excellent that you should have found work as tutor to the sons of so influential a family. Passing on to others the knowledge God has permitted you to acquire, you double your talent.

Have recourse to God in all your difficulties: in discipline, ordinary teaching, and the teaching of divinity. Your clumsiness in society and your inability to gain the love of your charges, provide lessons in the art of living, and are good for you as a counterweight to your preoccupation with theories. You are still very young and only beginning to try your wings in the great flight. Life itself must teach you, in one way and another, what is wrong, and what is right. Use your mistakes to encourage and develop your humility, and to increase your perspicacity and discrimination. Employ most of your spare time in reading the Greek and our own Fathers. No art is acquired easily or without much diligent study and practice. Could it be otherwise with the greatest art of all—the art of arts—the spiritual life, the soul's salvation? [377]

It almost sounds as though you had thought you could scale the ladder with giant strides! But take it from me, you have faith, you have indeed. If you had not, could you have seen through the enemy's machinations? But, on the other hand, you aspire after the higher and more consoling forms of faith, and this shows your lack of humility. Rest content with what has been given you; all faith is a grace, and God will give more when, and if, He finds fit.

When you fail, no matter in what, do not be trapped into agitation but, humbling your mind and heart, make penance and strive to keep our Lord's commandments. [378]

Every reverse is a pointer to some spiritual truth that we were in danger of forgetting. You should therefore strive calmly to settle down and examine, from this point of view, the reverse that has so deeply shocked you. [216]

You are distressed to find that whenever you now

examine your conscience, you see yourself as bad; whereas formerly, when you were young, such examination showed you to be, on the whole, good rather than bad. What an extraordinary reason for distress!

It is infinitely better for us to see ourselves as bad than good. In the first case, we acquire humility, and find the door to forgiveness, the door to grace; in the second, we grow proud; and pride blocks the way to grace.

As to the real value of our deeds and actions, of that God alone is judge; He, who knows the most secret impulses of every human heart. [396]

3. Discernment

Let us allude no more to the past but rather keep to what may be profitable in the future.

According to the teaching of the Fathers, any impression which, touching the heart,[3] fills it with a great agitation, must come from the region of passions. Therefore impulses which spring from the heart should not be followed at once, but only after careful examination and fervent prayer. God preserve us from a blind heart! It is well known that passions do blind the heart and screen the shining sun of the mind that we should all strive to gaze at. [41]

And so at last, the long period of eclipse is over; in your heart the sun shines bright, and in your mind the air is sweet and clean. Sweeter and cleaner than ever before. Praised be the Lord! This is a direct grace; though it is also, in a sense, the fruit of your own bitter sufferings.

But this new ability to pray is also a test; and so,

---

[3]The purified heart, according to the Eastern tradition, is the center of the rational will.

beware! If you permit yourself to relish the delight of your new ability, an even denser cloud of darkness than before will descend and envelop you. This is inevitable on the path we tread: delight in a spiritual attainment imperceptibly, surely, quickly draws us into the meshes of that great snare—spiritual pride. Then are we mightily humbled! And rightly; for we have proved incapable of accepting with pure gratitude a grace generously bestowed upon us.

Until humiliations have swept away all pride, any virtues we may laboriously acquire rest on a foundation of sand. It takes much time and requires great effort to build a foundation of rock, on which the art of prayer can securely thrive. [404]

Our quest for spiritual advancement cannot lead our soul *only* on to the meadows of joy and consolation, and leave it there. Sooner or later it is inevitably led on to the way of the cross. Carrying our spiritual cross we learn patience and docility.

You should definitely know that spiritual joys are always followed by a spiritual Calvary. [100]

4. Conformity with the will of God

Deeply moved as we are by your sorrow, yet what can we say? Open your heart, perceive the will of God. From Him seek help, in Him seek consolation.

Believe firmly: this tragedy is not the outcome of a chance concatenation of events. God Himself—God, whose ways are inscrutable—has confirmed them with the seal of His divine purpose. Why? Either as a punishment—but not necessarily for any sins of *yours*—or to try the power of your faith, and steel it. But whatever the reason, the whole occurrence is one more proof of His love of you, for *Whom the Lord loveth He chasteneth, and scourgeth every*

son whom He receiveth ... But if ye be without chastise-
ment, whereof all are partakers, then are ye bastards and
not sons (Heb. 12:6, 8). These are not words of our own
invention. It is the Apostle Paul himself who thus testifies
that you are a beloved child of God.

Strive hard for patient endurance! Do not weaken.
Hourly thank God for all. And He will see to it that good
comes of your right attitude.

Accept all, even this tragedy, as God's judgment: you
perfectly forgave this man; you refrained from inflicting
any punishment on him, but the judgment of God singled
him out, followed him, and struck him down. Who knows
what ways of helping evil in its dark work on earth he
might not have found, had he remained among us? But
now his departure is a frightful, chastening example to
multitudes. Had you sought to punish him, you would
have reason to condemn yourself. As things are, there is
no occasion for this.

We commit you to the protection of our Lord; may
He—who alone can—stem the source of your sorrows and
afflictions. [64]

The longing to seek God, to come near Him, is an
actual grace; it comes of our having, at last, heard His
call. And it is imperative that, having heard, we should
actively respond.

This we can only do by carefully keeping His commandments. No matter where we are and what our
circumstances may be: in solitude or in company, in a
monastery or in the world, everywhere and at all times
we must keep them, His commandments. This is never
easy: for, wherever we are and whatever our circumstances,
the enemy always tries to prevent us from actively respond-
ing to the call.

Pray for help. For help that you may never fail to
respond. And beware lest, having received help and having

done the right deed because of it, you should grow proud and acquire the habit of condemning others, in the secret chambers of your heart.

Beware! For this would make all the fruits of your good works wither. [92]

Since you clearly want me to be quite outspoken, I tell you frankly that I cannot think it right for you to leave the Service and restrict your activities to the peaceful, uneventful occupation of organizing and improving the life of a hundred men or so. Remember the parable of the talents.

Considering the benevolence that our Monarch is pleased to show you, who can doubt that you may be of much greater use to humanity remaining where you are?

You say, "At Court vainglory may seize me." It is good that you should fear this; but do not let fear grow into panic. Accept promotions gladly though humbly—not as food for pride but as an occasion to help others—listening carefully, all the while, to the voice of conscience resounding in your heart. God will not refuse His help.

As to this girl who has so much impressed you, why not marry her? You say you seek neither beauty nor riches but gentleness, intelligence, and devotion to the faith. The lady in whose house you met confirms your impression that she has all these qualities, and says she is well educated too. No mean advantage in a wife.

But, not daring to influence you in so important a matter, I can only recommend you to God. Pray that you may learn to read His will, and that, having read it, you may accept it.

If this marriage is agreeable to Him, your eagerness will increase after prayer. Then have a church service[4] said,

---

4Short occasional service of supplication, intercession, thanksgiving, or commemoration, called *Molieben* in Russian.

requesting the special blessing of our Lord and our Lady, and tackle the business straight away.

But if after prayer your eagerness wanes, accept this as a sign that God does not approve. Then drop the matter. [173]

You certainly have my deepest sympathy, but your own attitude to your misfortune will, in the long run, prove to be more helpful towards your regaining your poise than any feelings of mine could be. You are right: it is, of course, you yourself who have made the cross which you must now carry. A saintly man once said, "The wood of the cross that now breaks your back first grew in the soil of your heart." He was right.

Punishments are always harsh; but when accepted with humility, they bring us nearer God. And what else matters? If, under all circumstances, you carefully abstain from self-approbation on one hand, and from despair on the other, God will grant you His blessing. [331]

Once again you sink into melancholy and despair! Have you forgotten that the hand which chastises is also the hand that grants the greatest gifts? *Heaviness may endure for a night, but joy cometh in the morning (Ps. 30:5).* When we are incapable of scaling the peaks of virtue, all we have to do is to descend into the ravine of humility. Our humility is our surest intercessor before the face of the Lord. It is by dint of humility and penance that the last shall be first. Therefore take courage. [338]

Since God's will works in two ways, it does not bind us or make us unfree. Some things He desires; others He permits. This second way is made manifest when we insist on things happening as we think best. But when we docilely abandon ourselves to His will, He manifests the first, which is, ultimately, of greater advantage to us. [155]

5. Liberty of Spirit

When you must quickly come to a decision, and feel that you ought to have some advice on the point in question but have no one by you who could give it, turn to God as the Fathers teach us, invoking His help three times. [252]

God bless your decision to move into a new house, and may all go well with you there. But I cannot approve of this passion for smoking cigars. Just think, until recently you could call yourself a free woman, but now you are a slave, in bondage to a silly fad. Think too, how much money you squander on it.

Mind you, I do not forbid this indulgence; you must do as you choose. But my advice is: leave off. Leave off for your own good. [171]

Truly I have nothing at all to say to your lengthy descriptions of our Monarch's graciousness to you and your family, your gift of the icon, the incident with the portrait of the starets Seraphim, or to your opinion of the Bishop of Kiev. All these matters are far beyond the scope of a humble monk, weighed down with age, harassed by bodily and mental shortcomings, preoccupied by a ceaseless stream of ordinary hard work.

As to your daughter's wish, discuss it with her, not me. She is old enough to know her own mind. Question her, noting most carefully how she answers you. If her desire remains steadfast, if the sequence of her thoughts on this subject is unmuddled, and if she maintains perfect serenity throughout the whole discussion, you should look upon all this as true signs that God has stamped her desire with His seal. You should then definitely refrain from raising any more objections. Far from creating difficulties, you should give her your blessing. [50]

I understand that you now constantly torment yourself for having said during our talk, "Marriage—that were God's punishment!" Since your return home too, your friends and relations have been telling you that these words of yours must have greatly angered God because, through them, you showed your firm intention to build your life according to your own will, and not in accordance with His. They say, these friends and relations, that every wish and desire is sinful, and that you should fully abandon yourself to whatever comes along—God's will!

Do not seek truth or consolation in the richly garnished reasoning of worldlings. Seek them only in the Word of God. It is He, and no other, who bestows on man intelligence and free will. These gifts of His should be used in a constant valiant fight for betterment: your wish to dedicate yourself to God springs from this deep well of your free will.

When our desires, illumined by our own intelligence, are aimed at bringing about good—that is the will of God on earth—and when we act in accordance with this aim, God is well pleased and supports us. Even when, in a fit of wild madness, we wish to contest His will and strive to act in a manner that conflicts with it, He still refrains from breaking our will, and permits us to act wrongly, but freely. True, in the first case we reap our reward, in the second punishment, as is abundantly testified in Holy Writ.

But we only act true to our human nature when we ardently desire good, and persistently, valiantly strive to bring it about. This is no evil practice. It is nonsense to say that all desire is sinful, that we should never ask God to fulfil our wishes, that we should feebly abandon ourselves to what comes along. Surely, to act in this manner would be contrary to reason, to human nature, and to Holy Writ. Desire is not a sin; only the desire of evil is wrong. How could man belong to the kingdom of the Word, be a reasonable creature and free—if all desires were wrong?

And if you should now strive to wish for nothing, neither for a happy marriage nor for the purity of the virginal life, what kind of a life would yours be? You are not a log or a stone; nor were you ever intended to be. You were made woman, free to desire, choose, and act. [45]

There is no occasion to be afraid of praise; we must only guard ourselves against feeling gratified by it. St. Isaac tells us that such gratification, whenever felt by us, is in itself our full reward. But praise to which we are indifferent is harmless.

And do not agitate yourself over your resolution to read a litany daily at a fixed hour: this resolution which, you say, you now find impossible to carry out. To your question, "When it has been quite impossible to do so at the appointed hour, may I read it later, while knitting and minding the children?" I answer: No! this would be quite wrong. Our pledges are not debts owed to a harsh master who wants them carried out to the letter and cares for little else. The Lord does not wish to enslave us, He wants us free.

When you really cannot carry out a resolution, make penance, thinking of yourself as a humbled debtor. If you then refrain from the temptation of feeling agitated, it will be of greater profit than halfhearted mumblings followed by self-satisfaction and the pride of having kept your pledge in spite of all difficulties. [236]

The lives of men are subject to drastic changes. These changes are gradual at times; at others, lightning quick. But even those of us who enjoy long years of opulence and fame can find no consolation, no gladness, unless our heart is illumined by the steady light of peace. It is this peace that we must seek, it is for this peace that we should pray. The peace that our Lord gave to His disciples and to all those who really have faith in Him. . . .

You say your daughter and son-in-law are persuading you to go and live with them, and that you can come to no decision unless I give you my blessing and say that all will go well with you there and that you will be happy!

But how should I know anything about it? Who am I to say what will happen to you in this village or that town? I'm no seer or prophet.

All I can say is that I can hardly think this change, out of quiet into hubbub, will be of much profit to you. It is, of course, agreeable to be with those dear to our heart; but can this pleasure endure?

Still, I do not want to influence you either way; in this I want to leave your will quite free. I only pray that you may seek to blend it with God's will. [52]

II

Blessed are they that mourn: for they shall be comforted

1. Sorrow

I thank you for having unveiled to me the sadness of your grief-stricken heart; a great radiance comes over me when I share with others their sorrow. Complete, perfect, detailed compassion is the only answer I can give to your tender love of me that has led you, at such a time, to seek me out in my distant, silent, humble hermitage. . . .

Christ says, as it were: I accepted the cross for the salvation of mankind; and whomsoever I specially long to draw unto myself, on him do I first shower sorrows; his heart do I first pierce with arrows dipped in the wormwood of grief. This I do so that he may die to the extreme fascination, to the sweetness, of transitory joys and powers. The scourge of sorrows is the banner of my love. Thus did I wound the heart of my servant David; but when the stream of tribulations had separated him from the world, then did a dread meditation, an unwonted, blessed trend of thought well up in his mind and take full possession of his whole being. . . .

In the ground of the Christian's heart, sorrow for the dead soon melts, illumined by the light of true wisdom. Then, in place of the vanished grief, there shoots up a new knowledge made of hope and faith. This knowledge does not only wash the soul of all sadness; it makes it glad.

Fanaticism shackles the mind; faith gives it the wings of freedom. This freedom is apparent in a quiet firmness, unruffled by any circumstances, fortunate or unfortunate. The sword that cuts us free of shackles is the purified mind; the mind that has learned to discern the true, the secret, the mysterious cause and purpose of every occurrence. Purification of the mind is gained through frequently pondering on our utter insignificance; but this pondering should always be veiled in a throbbing, living prayer: for God's protection and His help. [47]

2. Failure

And so your good intentions have been frustrated by forces entirely outside your control. In the hard days to come, keep constantly in mind that God knows well how firm was your resolution, how keen your eagerness to act; and He may record your intention as having the value of an accomplished fact. He is particularly likely to do so if your humility remains quick, if it does not wither under the winds of adversity. Remember, too, that your careful tending of your humility can alone bring you consolation and peace.

And mind you do not let your faith grow dull. For even these great servants of God, the prophets, could do nought for them who lacked in faith. [83]

3. Poverty

Accept all hardships without grumbling. Be certain that they are your due. You yourself say that when you were young, rich, and in good health, your heart was callous and your mind empty. Since grown old, sick, and poor, you are kinder and more thoughtful, you have good reason to rejoice; none to despair.

But see to it that your poverty is not only a surface thing; see to it that you are poor in spirit too. Our Lord loves none better than the totally poor. [191]

The inexpressible and unaccountable melancholy that oppresses you and prevents you from enjoying anything may be a test, intended to prove the firmness of your decision and the purity of your love of God.

It is not joy of the spirit alone that manifests our love of God; unflinching courage, staunchly maintained through long periods of darkness and anguish, proves this love even more definitely. [393]

4. Bereavement

St. Paul does not forbid us to be *sorry after a godly manner (II Cor. 7:9)* but wishes us to grow in courage. Try to do as he says. [414]

5. Illness

When you see F. Y. give him my warmest greetings and best wishes for a speedy recovery. Tell him too, that even if his hope and faith are strong he should not despise the help of a physician. God is the creator of all men and all things: not of the patient only, but also of the physician, the physician's wisdom, medicinal plants and their curative power. [317]

With this letter Father X. will hand you a sugar basin that I have turned for you. If you should not like it, do not extend your dislike of it to me!

Being as weak in health as you are yourself, I cannot fail to feel much sympathy for your plight. But kind Providence is not only more wise than we; it is also wise in a different way. This thought must sustain us both in all our trials. And it is consoling, as no other. [223]

I am sorry indeed that your wife should be suffering from insomnia. This comes of her worrying so much about everything. Having myself been at one time subject to sleeplessness, I know how thoroughly exhausted it leaves you. The only certain remedy is to thrust away the whole lot of harassing thoughts and consciously to put everything in the hand of God, accepting His will in all.

But since this is more easily said than done, some simple devices may prove helpful: let her drink a glass of water before getting into bed, and put some bread near the bedstead—the smell of rye is very soothing. A good prayer to recite at such times is the prayer of the Seven Sleepers of Ephesus.[1] [435]

I was glad to hear that, strengthened by prayer, you underwent your frightful and most dangerous operation bravely, and without feeling—as had been feared—discomfort or pain. I rejoice to hear that, as your health improves,

---

[1]Maximilian, Iamblicus, Martin, John, Dionysius, Excutodianus, and Anthony—seven brothers, legionaries—came of an influential family of Ephesus. Arrested at the time of the persecutions decreed by Diocletian (284-305), they were thrown into a cavern, the entrance to which was so well blocked and concealed that their relations failed to find it. According to the written tradition they were unearthed in the fifth century, and "awoke very much refreshed." The rest of their life they devoted to the spreading of Christianity. This brought them to the notice of the Emperor Theodosius II (401-450), with whom they had occasion to converse. Their awakening is commemorated on August 4, their death on October 22.

the capacity of your soul deepens. It is good that you seek, and find, help and consolation in frequent communion. [116]

I was much pleased to hear from your relation how bravely you are bearing the cruel scourge of your heavy sickness. Verily, as the man of flesh perishes so is the spiritual man renewed. May God bless you and your family, and grant you peace and joy. [229]

Praised be the Lord that you accept your illness so meekly! The bearing of sickness with patience and gratitude is reckoned highly by Him who often rewards sufferers with His imperishable gifts.

Ponder these words: *Though our outward man perish, yet the inward man is renewed;* and: *If our earthly house of this tabernacle were dissolved, we have a building of God, an house not made with hands, eternal in the heavens (II Cor. 4:16, 5:1).* [113, 114]

III

Blessed are the meek: for they shall inherit the earth

1. Humility

"There is nowhere to hide from the host of temptations, except in the depths of humility." Do you remember these words? They are your own. [94]

Our war against the spiritual hosts of darkness is bitter indeed, since our enemy is mighty and never sleeps, since he is wily, cruel, proud, and yet fleshless.

All the more reason for us to enclose ourselves in the fastness of wise humility, alone impregnable to thieves and robbers. But while we are still far from having entered this fastness—this wise humility which is also perfect love— fear of God is our armor: *The fear of the Lord is a fountain of life, to depart from the snares of death (Prov. 14: 27).* [98]

You should know by now that great storms of passion are allowed to assail us whenever we have been indulging pride, self-adulation, high opinions of our own intellectual powers; or when we have pandered to the vicious pleasure of humbling others, intentionally. The medicine is simple: humility, a sincere humbling of self. This alone can bring relief: through meekness—the harbinger of peace. [393]

John Climacus has said: Love and humility form a

holy pair; what the first builds, the second binds, thus preventing the building from falling asunder.[1] [349]

2. Simplicity

Praise the Lord for all, thanking Him for His judgment no less than for His mercy; for the years of misfortune as well as for the hours of happiness. . . .

Your desire to say family prayers for your sick master is good; but your scruples about doing it in the right way are finicking. Pray simply: "Lord, have mercy upon our master and his family. Grant him a safe home-coming, good health, and peace of mind."

But see you pray humbly. If you should proudly think your prayer agreeable to the Lord and worthy of being answered, take it from me that it won't be heard. [419]

It is wrong to draw particular attention to oneself, during public prayer, through excessive kneeling or mistimed bowing.[2] Bowing and prostrations should only be performed during those parts of the service where they are customary. Then most of the people present will be doing likewise and no one will pay any attention to you.

As a rule, outward signs of emotion and tenderness should be mastered in public and the effort to master them offered to God as a humble sacrifice. [245]

As to your asking forgiveness (of those whom you have hurt) when you know that they will only mock and abuse

---

[1]*Philocalia*, II.

[2]Russian churches have no pews. The congregation mostly stand, and are free to kneel, bow, or make the sign of the cross. There is no obligation for everyone to do the same thing at the same time, but it is habitual for all to emphasize the most important words or moments of the service in one way or another.

you for doing so before your going to confession,[3] do not approach the matter so formally.

The first thing for you to aim at is a clear perception of your own misdeed. By the time you have attained to this, and true penitence has matured within your soul, these people may also have experienced a change of heart. But if you know that they have not and that they really will mock and abuse you, you should beg forgiveness of God in your prayers, and of them in your hushed heart. Then consider the subject closed and rest in peace. [240]

You seem greatly perturbed whenever you must touch upon the wrong actions of others in order to make your own actions clear. You are, in fact, so much perplexed by this necessity that you prefer altogether to omit mentioning the incidents involved.

Such scruples are unhealthy. When on due examination, you see that if you are to make the situation clear to me, you really must mention the evil deeds committed by others, do so quite calmly. You will not be judging these friends of yours or soliciting my condemnation of them, but only clarifying the situation so that your own perplexities and consternation may be relieved. If you tackle the matter with faith and humility, God will see to it that this relief is granted you. [239]

You ask if you may communicate twice during these

---

[3]An Eastern Christian usually sees his relations and closest friends before going to confession; he tells them of his intention and asks, in a general way, their forgiveness; he does not mention any particular offence unless there is a special reason for doing so; the answer has become a formula: "May the Lord forgive!" This custom is founded on two convictions. When men offend each other it is God that they offend; and it is to God that men confess their sins. But confession must be done in the presence of a priest, and can honestly be done only by him who can think that he is reconciled with all men.

seven weeks of Lent.[4] You not only may, but should. The Church tells us to go to confession and communion, at least once, even during the shortest lents of the church calendar.[5]

As to the difficulty of making your mind clear before confession, that should disappear if you face the matter with humility, without a trace of self-justification. Tune the whole of your heart and mind to the words: I have sinned, forgive me! Then, tell your confessor how you did it, and the load will roll away.

As I once told you, Peter Damascene explains how and why, after strenuous improvement and much practice of the Christian virtues, men at last come to see their sins spread around them as far, wide, and thickly as sand is at the bottom of the sea. This he describes as the first glimmer of light and the first flicker of humility. [235]

You say that, as far as your own failings go, you have calmly and fully accepted the new cross laid on you: the consumption that, the physicians say, has settled in your throat. But you go on to deplore the burden, the

[4]The longest fast in the Orthodox church year. Lasting from Vespers on the Sunday after Cheesefare Week till Easter Midnight Liturgy is over, it covers seven weeks of which the first, fourth, and seventh were kept more rigorously in Russia than the second, third, fifth, and sixth. In the nineteenth century there was no entertaining of any kind during the whole of Lent; everyone went to church; women of all classes wore high-necked dresses and no jewellery. In the twentieth century the general attitude towards Lent slackened. In St. Petersburg and Moscow some hostesses gave bridge parties and dinner parties; in the last years before World War I even dancing was not rare in the second, third, fifth, and sixth weeks. But there was still no entertaining of any kind during Holy Week.

[5]In the nineteenth century the majority of lay people went to confession and communion once a year, generally during Holy Week. This, the strictest minimum required not to lose touch with the Church, had come to be considered the rule.

nuisance, you have now become to others.

This is very wrong of you! Why think so disobligingly of others? Why assume that they are such bad Christians? I cannot think that they are so uncharitable as to treat a sick person as a nuisance. Surely, if they have ever read the Gospel, they must know that, when nursing you, they are, as it were, nursing Christ himself!. . .

With regard to your being ordered to eat ordinary—not Lenten—food during Lent,[6] I cannot possibly give you my "permission" to do so. We cannot permit what the Church forbids.

But here is my advice: accept this food as you do all other prescribed medicines. Then make your confession. Your confessor can remit a sin, once it has been committed and humbly confessed; and I have no doubt that he will. But neither he nor I can pick and choose in the wholeness of the Church's rules and, while insisting that you keep one, allow you to omit another.

Your chief concern, however, should be to achieve complete docility and ease of mind, even under these difficult circumstances. And there is no need for you to exhaust your weary body with spiritual exercises. Keep your heart open in praise of God, and thank Him for the cross He lets you carry. That is all you, in your condition, need do. [109]

Your so-called "daring," your gesture of writing with your blood a declaration always to serve God and the Community, is simply absurd.

---

[6]Eastern Christians are forbidden all animal food during any fasting season, not only meat and fish, but eggs (as coming from the hen), milk (as coming from the cow), and all milk produce. Thus—with the one exception of honey—fasting food is limited to vegetables, cereals, fungi, and vegetable oils. In the nineteenth century fasting was still strictly observed by Orthodox Russians.

Your divagations about pride and humility, and your wordy self-justifications, wander far from the point. John Climacus writes: Wherever we can note a fall, we may be certain that pride preceded it.

Not one of us can boast of having acquired humility: our actions, the whole of our life, prove the contrary. And where there is a lack of humility, pride is always present. Where light is wanting, darkness reigns.

Even when you take the oath to the Tsar, nothing as spectacular as this declaration will be expected of you. Can you really think our Lord rejoices in it? [123]

Can you really think that the inner peace you are seeking depends on the locality you finally choose to live in? Surely, inner peace is acquired only by humbly living in accordance with the commandments: *Learn of me: for I am meek and lowly in heart: and ye shall find rest unto your souls (Matt. 11:29).*

Where you do it is beside the question. . . .

In constant intercourse with other people we can sooner come to see our defects than we should in solitude. When, humbled through perceiving our ugliness of soul, we pray for God's help, we are never long left wanting. *He is our peace (Eph. 2:14)* and nothing but the grace of God can make of the human heart a heaven. [156]

You seem unduly distressed about your relations' disapproval of your actions. Why this great agitation? Since in all conscience you are certain of not being responsible for their hostile attitude to you, and since you are sure you have done nothing to induce them to feel or think as they do, be at peace. Be at peace and pray for them. We cannot persuade all that our actions are right, our motives pure. Everyone has his own way of approaching life, his own ideas on most things.

Offer up the whole of your actions as an offering to

our Lord. But in discussions on faith speak with humility, and not as a schoolmistress. [248]

Do not attempt to assess the quality of your prayer. God alone can judge its value. To us, our own prayer must always appear so poor an effort, so inadequate an achievement, that the cry of the publican spontaneously rises to our lips. [252]

3. Patience

Read Job and praise the Lord for all. When you have acquired enough humility, the punishment will cease. Until then, exercise your patience. Isaac the Syrian writes: Patience begets consolation, cowardice begets misery and pain.[7] [346]

4. Meekness

When people offend and mock you, remember that even this cannot possibly stand outside the pattern of God's providence. Take it as a pointer to your frailty, and as a sign that you should cure that frailty; take it, in fact, as the cure itself. It gives you an opportunity to exercise your powers of resistance, your strength to fight evil, your capacity to acquire humility.

I can well believe that it is not easy for you to live in the world. But until the Lord calls you and makes it possible for you to retire to a monastery, force yourself to live cheerfully, keeping His statutes and commandments; and guard yourself from condemning others for their lack of

---

[7]*Isaac the Syrian,* ed. Monastery of the Holy Trinity and St. Sergius, Radonezh, 1893, ch. 19.

zeal. The Lord is strong; He can see to their salvation and grant them the ardor to seek it, when, in His eyes, their time is ripe. [101]

Mr. Burachyok rightly says that the Lutherans[8] do possess gold (the Word of God) and silver (men with good dispositions) but that to this gold and silver they have added so much alloy (reasoning of proud, self-opinionated men) that the alloy has reduced the value not only of the silver but even of the gold. For this they bear responsibility and will have to answer. [241]

I was very glad to hear that you are so happy and so much at peace with yourself and others, now that you have become a member of our Church which has kept the Apostolic Tradition unbroken and unadulterated.

As to those people who are good and kind but are not believers, we cannot and must not judge them. The ways of the Lord are inscrutable; let us leave these good people entirely to His judgment and to the grace of His Providence. He alone knows how and why He has built the argosy of humanity, and the small boat of each one of us, such as it is.

Refrain from heated discussions on religious matters; there is no good in them. . . .

Be *not a forgetful hearer but a doer of the work* and you *shall be blessed in* your *deed (Jas. 1:25)*. But remember that growth in meekness is every man's greatest and most urgent work. [376]

Remember that *the carnal mind is enmity against God: for it is not subject to the law of God, neither indeed can*

---

[8]In Russia Lutherans chiefly lived in the Baltic provinces, annexed in the eighteenth century. But during the nineteenth century a considerable population of Russianized German Lutherans settled in St. Petersburg, Moscow, and other large towns.

be (Rom. 8:7). Therefore a man whose mind is not filled with faith and humility cannot be at peace; nor can the words in which he expresses his reasoning spread peace.

Learn meekness and docility from our Lord: *Learn of me: for I am meek and lowly in heart: and ye shall find rest unto your souls (Matt. 11:29).* [166]

5. Brotherly love

In the eyes of God, it is always preeminently right that a man should spend himself in devising new means for spreading consolation to his subordinates, who are his charges. [404]

Bear in mind that prayer alone, unaccompanied by moral improvement, is useless. St. Macarius of Egypt says of such prayer that it is unreal; that it is, as it were, a mask of the real prayer.[9]

As to your longing for solitude, bear in mind that, as Nilus of Sora tells us, it does not profit everyone. Our love of God finds expression in our love of men. And even when men hate us we should thank them for it, because they are then the tools of our correction.

When you are well satisfied, and consider yourself to be enjoying much grace, beware: the enemy never sleeps, and humility is the only weapon that shatters him. [105]

When, conscious of being in the wrong, you insist on justifying yourself before others and work yourself up into a state of great irritation, this comes, as you know, of your lack of humility.

---

[9]*Discourses, Epistles, and Sermons,* ed. Monastery of the Holy Trinity and St. Sergius, Radonezh, 1904; Discourse 3, ch. 5.

Strive to acquire humility. And charity—the real charity, which never limits itself to gifts no matter how generous, but, consuming the heart with infinite compassion for all creatures, generates a pure flame of good will and the firm decision to help every single one of the great host of unfortunates. [233]

IV

Blessed are they which do hunger and thirst after righteousness: for they shall be filled

1. Presumption

For enlightenment on the subject you are worried about, read the Commentaries of John Chrysostom:[1]

Faith is truly a gift, gained for us through Christ's advent. But this does not abolish our freedom or responsibility. God desires of us not only faith but action too. However, because of the prevenience of His grace which, through our conscience, summons us to be just and to reverence goodness, we have no occasion to be proud, either of our faith or of our works. . . .

When God, using our conscience, calls us to righteousness and yet our self-will opposes Him, He respects our freedom and lets our own will be done; but then, alas, our minds grow dull, our will slack, and we commit iniquities without number. On the other hand, the fruits of the spirit are soon granted to them who follow the commandments of Christ our Lord. . . .

Our penitence is only true and real when we decide never to revert to our sin. When we do not firmly make this resolve, our penitence is worse than useless. If we continue our indulgence in a sin, when we have already

---

[1]*Commentaries on the Gospels.*

recognized it for what it is and regret its hold on us, we show that we unreasonably count on God's readiness to forgive. This unreasonableness is quite as much to be condemned as despair. [51]

2. Repentance

You are, of course, quite right: there is no room for doubt! The Lord does indeed long to gather all into His arms. All—but particularly the worst sinners.

This truth must, however, be rightly interpreted, rightly understood: the Lord calls to Him all sinners; He opens His arms wide, even to the worst among them. Gladly He takes them in His arms, if only they will come. But they have got to make the effort of coming. They must seek Him, go to Him. In other words, they must repent. It is not that He rejects those who do not repent. He still longs for them, and calls them. But they refuse to hear His call. They choose to wander away, in some other direction. [78]

You say that whenever you go to confession, you are so feverish with fear that, losing your memory, you cannot collect your thoughts; you stammer or else stand dumb.

I conclude that when you appear before your confessor you are possessed by a great agitation. It is quite impossible to feel penitent, to be distressed about one's sins, in this condition. Beware: the enemy has found a useful weakness in you, and he is attacking you in your most vulnerable spot: your vainglory. . . .

We should go to confession filled with awe, steeped in humility, transfused by hope. Filled with awe, because we have offended God; steeped in humility, because we are fully conscious of the portent of our villainies; transfused by hope, because we are begging forgiveness of our loving Father, whose Son took up our sins and nailed them to the Cross, there to wash them with His own precious blood.

If you ponder this all fear should vanish. Fear is the backwash of that great agitation which springs from false shame blended with pride and vainglory. And it is this that overcomes you when you are confronted by the task of exposing the secret chambers of your heart to a servant of the altar.

Think of the publican and the prodigal son: you are both of them; and God is not only just, but also merciful. This should give you the courage necessary to regain your poise. But if you still find it difficult to remember all you ought to say, ask your confessor's permission to write it down, and glance at your notes during confession. There are examples of this practice in the teaching and life stories of the Fathers. [162]

An easy-going dismissal of our sins, the light-hearted decision that they are unimportant, betrays a lack of sensitiveness, a blind spot in the eye of our mind, a blemish of death in that which should be living.

As to this grief without reason that you say besets you, accept it as a spiritual cross. Accept it humbly, patiently, gratefully. The courageous bearing of this cross washes away our sins and frailties. Sometimes it even makes us perceive, at last, other sins of ours of which we were previously unaware. [177]

Since you diligently read the Gospels and the Fathers, you must know that no sin of ours can equal our Creator's mercy, let alone exceed it. . . .

If, at confession, you have been pardoned a sin committed in the past, it is unnecessary to mention it again. But it may sometimes be useful to ponder it, so that your repentance should not be dulled. See, however, that this does not lead to depression. If it should, drop it at once.

But try to combat the stoniness of your heart through intensifying your humility, not through calling forth tears; these are a special grace and should not be striven after. [191]

Without fear of God, beset by passions as we are, we cannot hope to accomplish God's will and train ourselves to love Him and our neighbour. *The fear of the Lord is a fountain of life, to depart from the snares of death (Prov. 14:27). . . .*

The three mightiest warriors in the enemy ranks are *the lust of the flesh, and the lust of the eyes, and the pride of life (I John 2:16);* when, aided by our self-love, they gain a foothold in our mind and heart, the portcullis of our soul is soon opened to a host of other sins and vices which then beset us on all sides and at all times. . . .

Beware of the usual temptation to think of God as abundantly lenient, before you have sinned; and to think of Him as wrathful, harsh, and unforgiving, after you have sinned. A sure way to despair, this is clearly a snare of the devil. [261]

Through your spiritual reading you have now come to see that you are weighed down under many heavy crosses, heaped on you by the world, the flesh, and the devil. And you are distressed, terrified.

Let not your heart be troubled! (John 14:1). Rather, rejoice. Think: you are no longer only a soldier of the Tsar but also a soldier of the king of Heaven. You have joined those who *wrestle not against flesh and blood, but against principalities, against powers, against the rulers of the darkness of this world, against spiritual wickedness in high places (Eph. 6:12).*

May despair never afflict you. In all extremities call out: *Save, Lord, I perish (Matt. 8:25).* And, while living in accordance with the commandments, keep strictly to the path of penitence and humility: the narrow path! [93]

3. Trust in providence

Listen! God Himself says, *Call upon me in the time of trouble; so will I hear thee, and thou shalt praise me (Ps. 50:15-16).* Afflictions confirm us in our faith, and teach us to set worldly glory at nought. Believe firmly that no suffering or sorrow can visit us—not a hair of our heads can fall—without God intending it. Although we are always inclined to put down our misfortunes to the ill-will or stupidity of other men, these are, in reality, only tools in the hand of God. Tools, used to fashion our salvation. Therefore take heart and pray to our Lord who is always at work for our salvation, using to this end both what we call happiness and what we call sorrow. [423]

Since your desire to attend church services is good, this overpowering anxiety about what may happen to your children while you are away from home can be nothing but a subtle temptation.

A father's presence in the home is naturally a great help to all; but since David the Prophet says, *The Lord preserveth the simple (Ps. 116:6),* can you think that your presence alone, without His help, is worth anything to them? On the other hand, surely His care is sufficient without your presence. And if God should allow some accident to befall one of them, could you prevent it, even if you were on the spot at the time?

When you leave home to go to church, commit your children to the care of our Lady and their guardian angels. In church, pray for them. But do not put off going there because of unreasonable scruples, anxieties and fears. [203]

To us, who firmly believe in Providence, even the most bitter adversities are but a movement of the hand of God; a movement of the hand of our Lord who is never weary of drawing man's attention to his personal way into the infinite; never weary of pointing out this way.

But for them who lack our faith the sorrows of this world are truly bitter. Is it to be wondered that the death of one they love leaves them disconsolate for life? [84]

Do not indulge despondency and distress if illness prevents you from going to church. The Apostle has told us that we ourselves are the temple of the living God.[2] Let that temple suffice you.

You, particularly, who say you receive special graces in church, should beware of spiritual pride, and recognize that you are now deprived of frequenting this source of graces because you are not worthy of them. The humbler we grow, the more firm and secure our spiritual life becomes.

Be active, of course; never cease being active; but do not hope to achieve much for your own salvation either by your works or by your merits. It is only the mercy of our Lord that saves us. [107]

Having learned of the calamity that has visited you, the temptations that beset you, I hurry to send a word of counsel and consolation. Was there ever a man who did not require the help of God and the support of fellow-men in moments of great sorrow? Even the wisest of us are, alas, inclined to lose clarity of thought and serenity of heart at such moments. . . .

Since you are not, and can in no way consider yourself to be, guilty of the crime you are accused of, accept this

---

[2] II Cor. 6:16.

visitation as a punishment for other wrongs that you *have* committed.

All that happens to every one of us is permitted by God. So you must realize that even this He has permitted; for your good, for the washing away of some of your sins. Strive calmly to review the whole of your life, seeing it of a piece as He does. Then, diligently uproot the evil you must, inevitably, discover after such an examination. And abstain from accusing others even in your most secret thoughts: accusations only destroy our peace of mind, they serve no purpose at all. [260]

None of your suffering has come by chance. Nothing can happen to us without our Lord's consent; and His consent is not only wise but always dictated by His love of us. Carefully examine your conscience and your life, and I am sure you will understand what I mean. Sorrow weighs you down? Never mind. The grateful heart, humble and wise—the heart which has become grateful, humble, and wise—will be greatly consoled and blessed with serene joy. [341]

To hold the faith does not only mean that we believe God to be our Creator. It also means that we recognize His unceasing and detailed attention to our good. This, however, our weak mind stifled by the gloom of our passions is, mostly, incapable of perceiving. . . .

It is not a dulling of ourselves under the downpour of sorrows, a schooling of ourselves in lack of sensitiveness, that we should seek, but the art of gratefully accepting and bearing sadness.

And remember: it isn't really the weight of this or that sorrow that overwhelms us. No, the onrush of grief is unsettling only to the unbalanced heart. Strive for the inner composition of peace. [42]

Do not worry about the future, the Lord is kind! Strive only to act strictly in accordance with His commandments in the present. And harbor no enmity towards any one, *Live peaceably with all men (Rom. 12:18).* [144]

4. Dependence on grace

When the enemy inserts despair into your heart, conjuring up in your mind thoughts of past sins so black that there can be no hope of pardon, refrain from weighing your own merits against your sins. Think only of the merits of Christ our Lord: the only merits that afford our salvation.

Remember, too, that Mother Church prays for all sinners, at every Eucharist. [110]

After a careful study of your disposition, which life has encouraged you to undertake, you have at last come to see that you have never loved; nor do you know or understand anything about love. And now you ask what is the best way to learn something about it. *I am the way, the truth, and the life (John 14:6),* said the Lord. And all His teaching is a teaching of love and meekness. But however we may strive to practice any of this, we must always remember that *without Me ye can do nothing (John 15:5),* and that even when we have done all the things that are commanded us, we can still only say, *We are unprofitable servants: we have done that which was our duty to do (Lk. 17:10).*

Our achievements must never loom large in our eyes; only our failures. But this must never lead us to despondency—the constant temptation—only to humility. . . .

We are told by our Lord humbly to bear *persecution.* Notice the word. He does not say the *punishments* we merit for our misdeeds. (That goes without saying.) But what He insists on is our gladly accepting *unjust* persecution for our good deeds. [243]

As I wrote before your last letter reached me, I cannot possibly come and stay with you just now; my Lenten duties are numerous and there is no one to replace me here.

Write and tell me all in detail. If you should find it easier to write as though it was another man's story, do so. I shall understand. Take courage. Do not fall into despair even in the darkest moments of the fight. But rather choose these specially to fling yourself on the mercy of our Lord, offering Him your stricken self and begging for His help. I warmly approve of your intention to go to confession at once and then to communion. [313: to the same correspondent as 312]

Praised be the Lord that Absolution and Communion have so completely healed you. But remember His words, *Behold thou art made whole: sin no more (John 5:14).* [314: to the same correspondent as 313 and 312]

5. Co-operation with grace

I cannot think why my saying that I am unable to help you without our Lord's succour and without your own effort should have caused you such consternation. How could I possibly assume that, on my own, I can be of any use to anyone? Actually, when asked to help, I pray fervently, recognizing the full weight of my sinful unworthiness, and fully aware that it is only in obedience to our Lord's command that I dare attempt anything at all. But even with God's concurrence, my prayers and efforts must still be of no avail if your will is not exerted.

Remember the story of the two kings, David and Saul.

Two most holy men prayed for them, Nathan for David, Samuel for Saul. And yet only David was forgiven. Why? Dimitri of Rostov[3] says it is because David fasted, wept and prayed all through the night, while Saul never thought of doing anything of the kind, but only sought distraction and amusement.

Now let us assume that because of God's grace, working through the sacraments of Penance and Communion, you yourself do obtain forgiveness for the past. So far so good. But the onslaught of evil will be renewed and, if you are not to fall even more pitiably than before, your will must be keyed to heroic resistance. Therefore I insist: if I am to help you your will must be exerted.

In your letters you go on to say that even when your will is set in the right direction, it is still hopelessly weak. That doesn't matter. Let this weakness be a source of humility, *Have mercy upon me, O Lord, for I am weak!* *(Ps. 6:2).* Resolutely steer the right course and hope for the best. Search the most hidden meanders of the dark labyrinths that surround the luminous core of your heart. And uproot pride wherever you find the weed.

When the dark passions seem to be getting the better of you, refuse to lose heart. Alone, you were weak indeed, but with God's help you are mighty strong. Steeling your own will to do His, humbly throw yourself on His mercy. If you do so, my prayers will be of the greatest help to you. [316]

---

[3]Born in 1657, in Kiev, of a Cossack family, Dimitri was professed in 1675, and soon came to be recognized as an excellent preacher. He left many writings (none of which are translated). He was appointed Metropolitan of Rostov (near Moscow) in 1680, died in 1709, and was canonized in 1752.

V

Blessed are the merciful: for they shall obtain mercy

1. Life in the world

I am glad that you have come to see that a life lived in the world can be as good, in the eyes of God, as one spent in a monastery. It is indeed only the keeping of God's commandments, love of all, and a true sense of humility that matter, wherever we are. [106]

2. Wealth

In ancient times, following the call of God, many men left the world. Using, with God's help, the weapon of humility, and following, with God's help, a rule of life entirely shaped in view of one end, they overcame all needs of the flesh. Requiring nothing of the world, they sought no riches. But their virtue attracted crowds of others, who hoped to find the way to salvation under the guidance of those who had forsaken the world.

Soon, mighty God-fearing princes sent treasures for the upkeep of the settlements. After much prayer, the Fathers would sometimes accept the gifts, distressed that this should entail the breaking of their vow of silence. But they never accepted any gift unless they had received a clear intimation that God wished them to: because of the multitude of souls which—both in the immediate and in the distant future—would thereby find salvation. . . .

Out of the fullness of their hearts, people bring to the shrines of saints some a pound, some a shilling, some a penny. The saints require none of this. And certainly God doesn't. But He gladly accepts the heart's pure impulse; that is always an acceptable sacrifice. [43]

I cannot approve of your intention to send your son to B. Nor can I understand why you should attach so much importance to the special commercial training he would get there. What is the point of learning how to make greater profits?

As I see it, he can very well be trained at home in everything that really is important. He need not leave home to become a good Christian, a kindly man, a respectful son. Nor need anyone wander abroad to learn prayer, and respect for the Church and for the servants of the altar. Are we more likely to acquire, far from home, the wish to work for the profit of our own soul and for the profit of the souls of others? Or to learn to love our neighbor? Or to be sober in all things? Or to lead a pure life? Or to resolve never to hurt another's feelings? Or to keep our humility alive and active?

You are quite rich enough as it is; your land not only provides an honest income for yourself and your family, but makes it possible for you to extend your charity to the needy. The tilling of the soil was blessed by God at the beginning of time. Be satisfied with the profit He sends you for your honest toil.

The small commercial business that has sprung up around it is quite big enough. Why seek to make this subsidiary side of your life grow? It is wiser to refrain from doing so. Remember: *They that will be rich fall into temptation and a snare, and into many foolish and hurtful lusts, which drown men in destruction and perdition. For*

the love of money is the root of all evil (I Tim. 6:9-10).
[208]

Living in the world, surrounded by your family, you cannot possibly give away all your possessions. So you must aim at finding the golden mean, and strive to keep to it: never turn your back on the world, but see to it that the world does not engross you.

All things that your children require you should carefully keep for them. Any surplus of any kind, give away to the needy. [233]

Your impulse to help these poor people, whose houses were destroyed by fire, is good. But it will remain good only if you temper your impulse with reason. And, although your help must be kept within reasonable limits, give your mite with a feeling of deep compassion. But, above all, be reasonable.

Even if you gave all you have, you could not properly alleviate the intense misery of them all. On the other hand, you have your family to care for and must strive to keep them comfortable, although it is right to dispense with all luxury for yourself and for them. But beware of the temptation to be unreasonably lavish. Besides, if you should follow this impulse on the spur of the moment, you would regret it later when it became clear that your children were doing without bare necessities. Then you would be well caught in the cauldron of a great and hopeless agitation.

Humble yourself and find peace. [238]

There is much on charity both in the Old and New Testament. God smiles on the compassionate heart. Every time a beggar knocks at your door, try to perceive Christ Himself under the humble disguise. Would you, under any circumstances, let Christ knock in vain?

The moral qualities of the individual beggar have nothing to do with it; that is Christ's concern, not yours. Who are you to judge your brother? Christ is using his hand and mouth to test your compassion of Himself. Will you fail Him?

But, rather than cut down your allowances to your poor relations, I should recommend careful examination of your own expenses, with a view to cutting down a multitude of unnecessary little luxuries. There is a large margin between this and "failing to live up to the requirements of your station," which is certainly not what you should aim at. This, a self-righteous form of shirking your responsibilities, would be quite wrong. . . .

Self-love is not natural to man. It is the result of original sin, which is contrary to man's true nature. [396]

3. Wages

I gladly give you my blessing. Do, by all means, ask your master to raise the pay of his workmen. Withholding, in one way or another, a decent living wage which would make the toilers' life bearable, so that they could praise the Lord for it, is a great evil which cries to heaven for vengeance. May these distressing conditions be eradicated in your concerns. God bless your decision. If you succeed, weary men will weep with joy on the eve of our great festival, and will join their prayers to mine for you and for your master. [427]

4. Work

I haven't time to write much but want to send you, without delay, a word of encouragement and my blessing.

It is certainly right that after much searching of the heart and mind, you have accepted this new responsibility.

If I had time I could quote endless texts to the point, but will sum them all up in these words: living in the world, benefiting by the worldly society of men, it is a sin to evade responsibilities and to thrust them on others.

May God constantly increase your wisdom and humility! I shall pray. [302]

I know the editor of the *Moskovityanin*[1] well. A religious and intelligent man,[2] he wanted religion, morality, and learning to be united in the pages of his journal. I upheld him in this, because I think such an effort particularly valuable at a time when the majority of people who call themselves learned are trying to tear religion and learning asunder. Unfortunately, ill health now forces him to do little himself, and he is obliged to leave most of the work to other, lesser men. [306]

Tell your wife that it is unreasonable of her to be distressed because your son finds his new job hard. Did not the Lord God say, *In the sweat of thy face (Gen. 3:19)?* Besides, what would happen if he did not work hard? Idleness begets many vices and he is of an age when the lusts of the flesh easily beset and overcome us. Arduous work often prevents this.

And if it is the lowliness of the job that distresses her,

---

[1] Monthly journal published in Moscow in the 'forties of the nineteenth century.

[2] Ivan Kireyevsky (1806-1856), one of the founders of the Slavophil movement. A follower of the Westerners in his youth, he met Hegel and Schelling during his stay in Germany, and remained under their influence for some time. But after his return to Russia and his marriage to Natalia Arbeniev—a "daughter" of Seraphim of Sarov—he abandoned German Idealism for the "Philosophy of Revelation," which he studied in patristic writings. About 1842, he placed himself under the guidance of Macarius, and soon became a frequent visitor to Optino.

tell her that she is suffering from pride, which she should busy herself uprooting. Tell her from me to rejoice, praise the Lord, and spend more time at prayer. All work is good, but prayer is the best work of all. [422]

I am glad that your wife is no longer upset about your son's work. It is excellent that he should be learning the actual work before training as manager. This will help him to acquire a right judgment on many problems which would otherwise escape him. A manager should have inside knowledge of the life of those whom he directs. [424: to the same correspondent as 422]

5. The life of religion

You say your incapacity to resist temptations, your slowness to conquer your passions, and your general moral debility depress you greatly, which only proves that you count on acquiring salvation by your own merits.

I, however, would have you bear this in mind: you—such as you are today—could perhaps rid yourself of every one of the sins that depress you; but only at the price of developing one that is the root of them all. And yet, the thought of this one has, apparently, never depressed you: because you have never suspected it was there. For good reason, it is your pride.

But look: if we are humble, God helps us to fight our sinfulness; if we are proud, He does not. And how can we acquire humility unless we are constantly humbled through seeing ourselves as we are—the worst of sinners? Unless we are constantly brought to our knees in penitence?

If our daily work—the constant fight against passions and inertia—did not keep us on the alert, we should come to live in an illusion of our sinlessness, joyously nursing our pride. And we would soon be wallowing in the abominable sin of imagined saintliness.

You may be sure that when you enter the monastery, and, particularly, when you are professed, this fight will grow even more intense; in order that, perceiving your utter worthlessness, you may work at uprooting your pride. . . .

You say that your father has at last consented to your becoming a nun. Praised be the Lord! You have my blessing for it too. But remember that this step must be taken with the utmost care. Do not tear the bonds that still unite you with your family and friends. Before cutting them, loosen them gently.

But the chief thing for you now is to pray that God's will may be done. Abandon yourself to it completely. [134]

Regarding your suggestion that your sisters' great distress, and the calamities that have befallen them, are the result of their not having kept the vow they made, I cannot say if this is so or not. But we must always remember how merciful a master our Lord is.

If it is true that they have failed to carry out their vow only because of circumstances that are beyond their control or for lack of money, they should do penance, disclosing the whole situation to their confessor. Do not doubt that the Lord will pardon them.

But it may be as well for them to ask their confessor for a dispensation from this impossible undertaking. He could easily substitute for it another, to be carried out as an obedience. This may be best, in the long run. [211]

Do not think that even here any one of us constantly enjoys consolation. No: here, as everywhere, flesh and mind are at war; here as everywhere, there is falling into pride and purification through humbling: here, as everywhere, we long for consolations but must learn to carry a weighty cross. This cross tests our love. Can we, do we love God even under the weight of the most bitter adversities? [92]

Your condemnation of the nuns of X. is as wrong as your ideas on monasticism are erroneous. The call to the Life does, of course, come from God, although we accept it in full freedom to save our souls. But in order that men may recognize their spiritual sores, they require long tests, many temptations, and bitter sorrows; all of which purifies the heart and restores health to the stricken soul, sundered from the All-Good at the time of the Fall. Therefore monasteries are not, and cannot be the "quiet havens ringing with prayer and filled with calm, unruffled obedience" which you imagine them to be. This illusion of yours is an ugly one indeed, since such an existence were a mechanical one, far from perfection and in no way leading to it.

Although you can know nothing of the sinister temptations and grim fight waged by religious, you may get an idea of what I mean if you carefully read the four first Rungs of John Climacus. In practice, you will never know any of this, and there is no need for you to study it in detail. Still, it is good to try to see that, reacting rightly to such gossip, religious may use it for their own betterment and turn it into a weapon of perfection. Some of us cannot attain to simplicity, meekness, and humility without the help of sharp shocks: such gossip, spread by scandalmongers, and the actual fires of which such gossip is the greatly exaggerated, lurid smoke. . . .

But your immediate concern should be with yourself. Strive hard to be a Christian wife and a Christian mother. This is not easy. If you do strive for it, you, in your world, will find as many snares and pitfalls as we do in ours. Yours may be of a different kind but they are no less difficult to evade. Remember always that, once we have decided consciously to strive after righteousness, we cannot escape catastrophes and sorrows, no matter where we are. [251]

You have accomplished one of the tasks set before the faithful: filled with admirable zeal, you not only visited the shrines of saintly men and women, but devotedly followed the steps of our Master in the Holy Land.

Through all these efforts you acquired great spiritual treasures, and the hardships and temptations that now beset you are apparently intended as a test. Prove, through bearing up manfully, that you really have made these spiritual treasures completely yours; prove to yourself and us that nothing can wrest them from you. Accept this visitation with gratitude and whole-hearted composure. You will soon perceive that the treasures you had formerly acquired now shine with a new brightness. [222]

Do not exaggerate the blessings enjoyed by those who frequently visit us; abstain from rashly concluding that your own work prevents you from coming here because, in God's eyes, you are "unworthy of obtaining grace."

Everyone who comes here receives spiritual benefit according to his faith. Those whose faith is poor find little benefit, and, sometimes, none at all. On the other hand, God is the Lord of all places. Now—since the Incarnation— Jerusalem is no longer the only sanctified spot; the whole earth shines with glory; there is no place whence the incense of prayer cannot rightly rise. The manna of the Word of God rains down on every city and every wilderness; the incorruptible feast can be partaken of in the humblest church of the poorest village; the living waters of grace can be drunk by all who courageously and unflinchingly seek Him who says, *If any man thirst, let him come unto me, and drink (John 7:37).* [299]

VI

Blessed are the pure in heart: for they shall see God

1. Passions

Your reasoning on the passions is entirely false: God has armed us with intelligence and a free will; His law, when followed intelligently and freely, becomes our shield. We must keep our arms polished and use them courageously in our two unceasing wars: our offensive war, the fight to understand and follow His law; and our defensive war, our resolution never to succumb to that which is contrary to His law; the law being nothing but His expressed will.

For, alas, no sooner does a man break God's law, than he is spiritually punished: having lost grace, he eats away his heart in vain longings, endeavoring all the while to choose for himself the best of many equally bad things. These longings and endeavors deflect his attention away from his real good, and dim his intelligence. Soon, having become the slave of his passions, he can no longer resist their lure; then the mead of pleasure changes to the sting of retribution.

Our passions are indeed our most pitiless tormentors. So unrelenting are they that even the humbled sinner who, having recognized them for what they are, wishes to free himself of their domination and decides to leave them and face the light, even though he is still tormented and tortured by their murky brood. They pursue him long.

77

They crowd around the unfortunate until his constant resistance to their renewed attacks and his active penitence have wiped their very memory from his heart.

On April 1, read the life story of Mary the Harlot. [53]

2. Anger

I was distressed to learn that you are still as irritable as ever. Fear of God, love, and humility are the medicine. Pride is the root of this besetting passion of yours. Read Mark's Epistle to Nicholas, in *Philocalia* I. [385]

You say your maid annoys and irritates you so much that, in order not to fly into a rage, you have taken to telling her—whenever you feel a paroxysm coming on—that she must not lead you into temptation, after which you hurriedly leave the room. This seems to me a remarkably weak way of combating the root of the evil.

Consider her, in this connection, as being used by God to show you your greatest weakness: this rage which slumbers in you at all times but lies hidden until she, the hand of God, discloses it. Combat this temptation through practicing humility, charity, courage. It will take long to conquer; but pray for help and start now. [397]

Your flying into a rage whenever the children fail to grasp your meaning, or when they misbehave, is of course a great fault. You must fight hard against this passion which is apparently getting you into its clutches. Read John Climacus; he deals with anger and meekness.[1] John Cassian[2] and Nilus of Sora are also most illuminating. [379]

---

[1]*Philocalia,* II.
[2]*Ibid.*

Guard against despondency. Courageously fight your fits of rage; never despair of overcoming them. This rage is one of your worst passions, but you could not wish to cure yourself of it if you did not see it. Therefore, the children who call forth these fits are God's instruments for your correction. Thank them for it, in the core of your heart.

Refrain from reprimanding them while you are in this condition. It will be better for you, and more impressive for them if you talk things over calmly, a little later. [383]

You are quite right: it was wrong of you to stand up so hotly for your husband. This inclination of yours to be carried away on a wave of blind rage whenever you defend those you love, shows a blemish in you.

But the perception of a blemish must never lead to despondency, only to penitence. Humbly confess to God this sin, this dark passion, this rage of yours; and pray for His help, so that you may gradually learn to defend with a magnanimous, firm gentleness even those whom you love best. [231]

You ask for some way of completely eradicating irritability. The inclination to irritability is given us to use against sin, and we were never meant to use it against our fellow men. When we do, we act contrary to our true nature.

We use irritability in this wrong, deflected way because we are proud. You must, of course, strive to curb your irritability; but guard yourself against being elated if you succeed. Read John Climacus,[3] and John Cassian.[4] Also Nilus of Sora. [238]

---

[3]*Ibid.*, Rungs 2 and 24.
[4]*Ibid.*

3. Hatred

It is good that you should be at peace with all but one; distressing that you should be unable to bring the breath of peace between yourself and this one. Who can boast of being without frailty? Not one of us.

The enemy constantly endeavors to awaken in the abyss of the human heart a great turmoil about trifles. This is one of his tricks to blind our soul to the sun of truth, Christ our Lord, hidden in the heart's core of every one of our neighbors. [71]

I greatly rejoice to hear that, with God's gracious help, you have actually overcome your fierce temptations and trials.

These bitter memories which, you say, stick in your heart like a great rusty nail, no matter how you hate them and try to pull them out, reveal the content of your moral make-up. Contemplating this rankling nail, recognize your frailty, humble yourself, and pray that God may help you to eradicate from your heart all bitterness and hatred, and that He may restore peace to your family life.

Since you are preparing to visit the Holy Land, it is important that you should regain your serenity. May the Lord help you to do so. May He help you to foil the enemy's intention of subjecting you—now more than ever—to the turmoil of a great agitation. [280]

4. Pride

Constantly bear in mind that, in the eyes of God, a penitent sinner is preferable to a proud man who has not sinned otherwise than by his pride. . . .

Whenever our prayer subtly conceals that sharp icicle,

our pride, it acts as a poison and can only lead us further away from God. [145]

"But," you may well ask, "what means are there of acquiring humility?" Well, we acquire this art through reading the Fathers; pitiless self-examination and self-accusation help too; also, making clear to ourselves how much worse we are than others; and refraining from all condemnation of them while we accept all their condemnation of us, as sent by God to cure our hideous spiritual sores. [146]

Bear this in mind: the Christian life is an unending spiritual fight. The wily enemy cleverly uses snares and arrows without number. Before some of us he spreads the lure of worldliness, the outer pride of pomp and circumstance, the cruder lusts—the lusts of the flesh.

But those of us who are not attracted by any of this he leads up on to the peaks of subtler prides. Having got us there—to the high country of self-esteem—he causes a dark mist, the mist of the subtlest prides, to enshroud our intellect. Then he leads us, his blinded slaves, away from God, without our even suspecting it.

Mark this too: it is not very hard for the simple sinner to come to hate his foul life and, leaving it, to fling himself on the mercy of God; but it is very hard for the subtler sinner—the self-sufficient one—to let a ray of divine love pierce the leather jacket of his self-righteousness. . . .

Humility is the only weapon that wards off all attacks, but it is difficult to fashion, and the art of using it is often misunderstood, particularly by those who lead an active, worldly life. [72]

I can assure you I have not the slightest suspicion that you are seeking to hide any detail of your life from me; nor have I ever thought you double-faced. But I cannot

81

fail to see how subtly you contradict yourself, how you misunderstand and misinterpret yourself. Remember always that the whole of our human misery is the consequence of pride. Humility alone is the path to joy, the gate to the blessed nearness—the intimacy of God.

John Climacus[5] relates that a saintly old abbot once set about curing one of his spiritual sons of the vice of pride. When the old man at last ceased speaking, the young one meekly remarked, "Forgive me, Father, but of this vice of pride there is no trace in me." To which the old man retorted, "And what do you think could better prove its hold on you than these proud words, advanced so meekly?" [73: to the same correspondent as 72]

5. Temptation

Remember that a good action is always either preceded or followed by temptations. God permits this so that the virtue, exercised in that particular action, may be confirmed, consolidated, steeled. [240]

You complain of overpowering laziness. This temptation often besets those who take on spiritual labor. To get rid of it the Fathers advise us to hold death constantly before the mind's eye; death with its two alternatives, eternal torment or eternal bliss. The Fathers say that this, when carried out with perfect humility, brings down upon us that grace which completely frees us from laziness. [226]

So now, our charitable Lord has, in an unforeseeable manner, unravelled the complicated knots of your dark temptations, simultaneously granting you the courage to

---

[5]*Philocalia,* II, Rung 23.

accept with gratitude all that the future may hold in store. Thus is the heart of man helped to die unto the fierce lure of the world; to be rid of every hankering after vainglory, every attraction of sensuous excitement, all lust after gold and silver. [48]

You are sorely distressed because of the surge of blasphemous thoughts against our Lord that you cannot stop. Believe me, you are innocent of these blasphemies. It is not you, but the devil who invents them. You do not take part in making them up and you are not responsible for them. But when you are overcome by distress he is delighted, and quickly unfolds an even richer carpet of them before you.

My advice is: firmly refuse to accept his suggestion that these thoughts are sins of yours. Strive to regain your poise, strive for peace of mind. Then they will soon vanish altogether.

Blasphemous thoughts assail us when we settle down in the comfortable illusion that we are living as we should, that we are getting on nicely with warm, fervent prayers, and when we condemn others for their lack of zeal. It is in punishment for such sins as these that the devil of blasphemy is allowed to creep into us.

Think less of yourself, refrain from judging others, and, with God's help, evil thoughts will lose their hold on you. I shall pray that they may soon do so. [176]

Be careful not to undertake more rigors than you can bear. And since you are troubled by evil thoughts, remember that a simple evil thoughts is not a sin but only a test of the quality of our free will. We are free to indulge it or thrust it away. But whenever an evil thought becomes entwined with the corresponding passion, we *have* sinned and must make penance.

When we are not strong enough to fight unaided

against such compound evil thoughts, we should pray for help to our Lord and our Lady. And, since pride is always the ground on which these battles are won by the evil thoughts that have crept into us, the most important thing is thoroughly to humble ourselves. [237]

St. Isaac says that whenever a man properly humbles himself, grace gathers round him.

You long for peace of mind, peace of the soul, but cannot find it? Of this peace—always a great reward—our Lord Himself says where and how we are to seek it: *Take my yoke upon you, and learn of me: for I am meek and lowly in heart: and ye shall find rest unto your souls (Matt. 11:29).*

None can achieve this except through battling with temptations and through suffering great sorrows. Our Lord, too, fought, suffered, and sorrowed much before the time of His death on the cross. He was reproached, vilified, humiliated, and tempted. And He laboriously built up for us a picture of His own life on earth, which all of us must strive to follow. Read St. Isaac, Chapters 78 and 79. There you will learn how necessary temptations are, and that they are permitted so that we should gain strength in fighting them. He chiefly examines temptations of the spirit; but what he says also holds good for temptations of the flesh.

As warriors are awarded medals and crosses for repeatedly proving their readiness to sacrifice their lives, so we—soldiers of the spirit—can only reap our reward after fighting valiantly and long. The greatest fight of all is the fight against pride, with all its symptoms of anger, vainglory, rage, hatred. When we have overcome this, we receive our best reward: the beautiful peace of the soul. [212]

Your description of your new ailment, this storm of

dark passions that has swept away all traces of your hard-won peace, wrings my heart. My compassion for you is great; but it were idle for either of us to think that I can give you any help without the succour of our Lord, and a great effort on your part—an effort into which you must be prepared to throw the whole of your will.

Remember what I have often said: pride is the forerunner of every fall. Since you ignored and refused to fight the devil's brood in its infancy, you are now beset by a mature host grown to the stature of giants. But with God's help all battles can be won. Appeal to Him constantly and, in your most bitter moments, fling yourself at His feet calling out as the Prophet did, *Have mercy upon me, O Lord, for I am weak! (Ps. 6:2)*. The grace of God can bring about what nothing else could.

May we humble ourselves, refrain from all condemnation of others, and accept in a spirit of love and devotion all that God sends for our betterment. [315: to the same correspondent as 316]

When beset by temptations pray for courage and strength to remain firm. Remember: there *is* an eternity! [264]

VII

Blessed are the peacemakers: for they shall be called the children of God

1. Man and Wife

The most important thing in your letter is one that you never stress, one on which you ask no instructions, one which you never formulate clearly, but which comes out in every line: the growing hostility between you and your wife.

I see little hope of this poison being cast out of your home unless you promptly cease condemning each other. You clearly think you are always in the right; she, of course, thinks she is. You heap on her a multitude of grave or petty accusations. She does the same to you. Where will this end?

Your chief accusations against her are touchiness, conceit, an absurdly exaggerated opinion of self. But, surely, if these were not your own most prominent defects —which they quite obviously are—you would not be so greatly irritated by perceiving them in her. Beware of your own failings!...

All this financial trouble between you comes of your having completely forgotten that yours is a Christian home, or should be. A home is a Christian one, when all the members of the household bear each other's burdens, and when each one condemns only himself. You have forgotten this, both of you. And so every word of hers pierces you, like an arrow dipped in poison. And your words, likewise, pierce her.

Ponder the truth of Christian marriage: man and wife are one flesh! Does it not follow that they must share all their possessions? And yet you two haggle over this property! And why? Because of words!

Unless you promptly strive for, and achieve, a loving peace between you, it is hopeless to try to bring tidiness and fairness into your business dealings with one another. Humble yourself, not her. Love her, not yourself. [75]

I need hardly tell you how wrong it is, this frigid attitude of yours to your husband. You describe it as a subtle, hidden revenge for his past indifference to you; and you are, yourself, quite clear about its being a sin. But, surely, having seen this and stated it, you must on no account accept the situation as inevitable, saying, as you do, that although you deeply regret it you can do nothing about it. This cannot be true, and is a very wrong attitude to take.

Remember what marriage is: a sacrament! Remember that the first obligation of man and wife is to love each other and be completely loyal to each other under all circumstances, to the end of their days.

Is it against this man to whom—in God's sight—you owe the wholeness of your love and loyalty, is it against him that you have nursed for long years—and are still nursing—an evil feeling of cruel revenge? Pray that you may be given the strength to forgive all those who have trespassed against you and that your own trespasses may be forgiven you. [124]

It is indeed hard to be forced, as you now are, to choose between two actions both of which are, strictly speaking, wrong, each in its own way. If you give this money to your husband, you will break the commandment of obedience to parents—since your mother expressly forbade you to do so; if, on the other hand, you refuse it him, you will violate the great mystery of matrimony in which a man leaves his father and mother to cleave to his wife; *and they two shall be one flesh (Eph. 5:31).*

In cases of this kind, when one of two commandments must be broken in order that the other may be kept, the Fathers counsel the breaking of the lesser. No connection on earth is greater than that between man and wife. It is therefore right that you should stand by your husband no matter what happens; and none can forbid you sharing all with him. All, not only your money.

The necessity to keep this gift secret, so that your mother should not vent her anger on your husband and cause even greater complications in the family, is another source of anxiety for you. And yet it is right to bring about and maintain peace!

Give your husband all he wants, and say nothing about it. But be fully conscious of your sins: the act of disobedience and the furtive action. Humble yourself, and pray for pardon. But do not lose hope that it will be granted. God is a reader of hearts, and permits such situations so that we may not lose humility while striving for perfection. . . .

The joint prayer of husband and wife is a great force. That may be one of the reasons why the enemy is trying to get both of you to break this excellent habit. One more temptation which God permits so that you should learn to overcome it, and come out of the testing stronger than before! Remember that, under all circumstances, humility is your surest weapon. [254]

89

2. Mother and Child

I can only say that, between you, you have bound me hand and foot. How am I to give you advice? If I say that I think this marriage right, I shall hurt your mother's feelings and shall be inciting you to act against her wishes: this I in no way wish to do, since you most certainly owe her filial obedience. But if I say I think this marriage wrong, I have your assurance that you will die of it!

Besides, I wonder: will my saying this or that be of any use? I doubt it. And I think that, under the circumstances, the *only* thing any of us can do is to pray that God's will may be done.

If He intends that you should be this man's wife all hindrance will be overcome, and marry him you will. But if God does not wish it, no matter how you plan and strive for it, will be of no avail.

And beware you do not blindly insist that things must work out according to what you consider to be right and good. God sometimes does permit such blind insistence to be followed by the fulfilment of our ardent desires. This always leads to misery and disaster (intended to open our eyes on our folly), and happens particularly often when our desires are founded on wild passions.

Pray to our Lord for guidance, and to His Holy Mother for special protection. [122]

It is very wrong that you do not love your mother, and harbor this feeling of suspicion against her. Pray for the strength, the courage, the goodness, to forgive. You must stop these endless recriminations, this reverting to— this endless dwelling on—her mistaken attitude to you in the past. Accept that past as part of God's pattern for your life, and forget your grudge. Forget it all. In keeping keen within you this hostility to your past and to the tools that shaped it, you are only waging war against the will of God. What folly!

Besides, you cannot honestly consider your fate to be a hard one. There have been bitter moments, I know. But, surely, the right thing to do is to forget them and train yourself to think of no one as their author, of no one as the one person responsible for them. Seen from on high, men are nought but instruments in the hand of God.

But take courage: God will reward you for humbly laying bare the ugly sores of your soul before another sinner. He will grant you the strength to overcome your sins. . . .

Do not misunderstand me: I am not denigrating your rule of prayer, or your reading of the Fathers and Doctors of the Church. I want to leave you quite free to continue these occupations or to modify them according to your own light. But do try to remember that love of the neighbor is the first *work* you must strive for. And you do not even have to leave your house to find that neighbor: your husband is that neighbor; your mother is that neighbor; and so are your children.

And do not let the dryness of your prayers depress you. Only the humble may safely be spared it. [124]

I am very glad to know that you have come to see this hidden pride of yours. You are acquiring humility, and our Lord looks with favor on all who are humble.

But you exclaim in horror, "What must I look like in the eyes of God!" What *did* you think? Surely not that He sees you as good, pure, and sinless.

And what nonsense is this about not having children? Children are one of the many blessings God has bestowed on man. As for woman, the Apostle says, *She shall be saved in childbearing (Tim. 2:15)*. It is for God to decide whether you do or do not have children. Accept them gladly if He sends them; do not sorrow if He doesn't; but don't presume to pick and choose, or interfere.

And strive to combat this jealousy and suspicion. There is probably no ground for any of it. The mind of those who are given to jealousy breeds the most improbable fantasies, because the devil gladly paints convincing pictures which have no foundation outside his imagination and theirs.

P.S.—Your letter telling me of your little daughter's death has just arrived. I have already told you how wrong it was to pray that you should not have children. But it is quite as wrong to suppose that this could in any way lead to her death. No, you certainly are not responsible for it! The Lord has taken her to Him not because of anything you did, but because He wanted her in heaven, by His side. Seek strength and consolation in the faith that she is even nearer to Him now than she was in life, and that she is now entirely in His care. [242]

3. Father and Child

Forgive me for not answering sooner, but my table is covered with unanswered letters, and many of them are as full as yours of descriptions of this new and growing visitation, this enmity between members of one family: parents and children, brothers and sisters, and so on.

I had written to your children before I heard from you, and said all I thought right. But I doubt if my words can have any effect on those whom the word of God leaves cold and unimpressed. It is this growing indifference to His word and our consequent refusal to examine our hearts— where we could find both the peace He bequeathed us and insight into our lack of love of Him and of our neighbor— which brings in its wake this punishment, this disruption of the home. [375]

I know that you are charitable and that many have been royally helped by you. But today Christ the wanderer, Christ the beggar, is knocking at your door hand in hand with your own granddaughter, surrounded by her six little children. Listen: He is begging! Begging that you should provide Him with a roof under which to rest His head! Buy a house for them: a small house, worth three to five thousand rubles. A trifle for you. But Christ will be so grateful for it!

He will be so grateful that His angels will straightway set about building you a mansion in heaven: a golden mansion. Three to five thousand rubles for that!. . .

Think, this is Christmastide. Is it not the season, above all others, in which to exercise fatherly love? Give this great consolation to your child. Give a home to the wandering, to the begging Christ. [138]

4. Brother and Sister

Try to blame yourself, yourself only and not your relations, for all. Be certain that none can offend or hurt us without God's permission; and whenever God permits it, it is always for our good. Punishments, tests, temptations, are all equally good for us.

You may ask your brother for help; but do it courteously, gently, without insistence. Besides this, pray, have faith, and abandon yourself—and the whole pattern of your life—to God. Pray fervently that peace may be restored in the family. [413]

Although I have not the honor of knowing you personally, I have heard so much from your distressed townsfolk about the exemplary life your family led during your father's lifetime and of the bitter enmity which now divides you, that I am writing to beg you to come to your senses.

Stop these endless quarrels and bitter insults! Do not provide the enemy with this delight: he enjoys nothing better than the distortion of family life, the mockery of it.

Remember that you are pupils of Christ; of Christ who teaches us to love not only our friends but even our enemies, and to forgive all who trespass against us. *But if ye forgive not men their trespasses, neither will your Father forgive your trespasses (Matt. 6:15).* What a frightful prospect!

And so, I beg of you, leaving all recriminations, make peace among you and strive for the greatest boon of all: strive for the inner peace. [210]

5. Children

Have great care of your children. We live at a time when much freedom is given to the expression of thought, but little care is taken that thoughts should be founded on truth. Teach them to love truth. [235]

VIII

Blessed are they which are persecuted for righteousness sake: for theirs is the kingdom of Heaven

1. Prayer

I am amazed that without knowing me—or knowing me only by hearsay, and rumors are so often false, you should seek my advice. But I dare not doubt God's love of the seeker; a love which, according to Holy Writ, often causes the right words to come even from the mouth of dumb creatures, creatures that don't even belong to the kingdom of the Word. And so I shall answer you, to the best of my ability.

Never having seen you, and having only a scanty written description of your circumstances, I can hardly have a true, full picture of your heart and mind. But one thing seems clear enough: notwithstanding your imagined great improvement you are entirely lacking in inner quiet and peace. I consider as an outstanding improvement this great love of God to which you so frequently refer. You go so far as to say, "I love Him so much that I simply cannot describe how much I love Him."

I only wonder if you haven't forgotten that love is the summit of perfection, and comes to us through our living in accordance with God's will and commandments. Read John 14:21 and 24. Also I Cor. 13:4-8. To this you may retort that the Apostles had in mind only love of men, whereas your love is of a superior kind—it is no less a thing than love of God! But is there any love of God where there is no love of men? Can there be? Read John 4:20 and Luke 17:10. Strive for humility! Humility, without which no virtue is true in the sight of God. Indeed, humility and love are so closely bound together that we never find the one without the other.

In your inner make-up I detect fear, doubt, and turbulent agitation. These can only reign in them who have not yet blended the whole of their being with the sweet breath of humility. Read Matt. 11:29 and I Tim. 1:15. The Apostle Peter was always conscious of his sins, and says so; many saints, too, considered themselves great sinners. This, however, did not wake any trace of agitation in their hearts: they had never counted on their own virtues bringing them salvation; they counted only on the achievements and mercy of Christ our Lord.

You proclaim yourself to be a gross sinner, yet you insist on your outstanding merits; and with it all, you disclose this great agitation. Indeed your inner make-up prevents you from perceiving the light of wisdom, prevents it from irradiating you.

You say, too, that at home you pray most beautifully, with the greatest, sweetest profit to your soul; but that in church you cannot pray fruitfully.

Do you not understand that this is a great temptation, fed from the same bitter source that makes your peace and quiet wither?

Be sure that when, in solitude, you pray in a manner which calls forth the sweetness and the tears that you delight in, God is ill pleased. Be sure that sweetness and tears, unaccompanied by a sense of the deepest humility, are nothing but temptations.

Having succumbed to them at home, and not finding them at your beck and call in church, you conclude that church-going is useless to you. Then you become a prey to bitter depression. But this depression is, in reality, the fruit of your prayers at home: the tempter first hurries you to the crest of the wave, then hurls you down into the trough. It is because you indulge pride that you are so vulnerable.

Pray simply. Do not expect to find in your heart any remarkable gift of prayer. Consider yourself unworthy of it. Then you will find peace. Use the empty cold dryness of your prayer as food for your humility. Repeat constantly: I am not worthy; Lord, I am not worthy! But say it calmly, without agitation. This humble prayer, unlike the sweet one you delight in, *will* be acceptable to God. [55: to the same correspondent as 72 and 73]

Guard yourself against muddled thinking on mental prayer.[1] As you can find out for yourself in the abridged life of Gregory of Sinai,[2] it took the Orthodox Church very long to perfect its method of mental prayer. In fact, the Church was hardly less slow in this than in completing the development of her rites, which took seven centuries. It is, therefore, not at all strange that Basil the Great should say nothing about it.

Even when the practice of mental prayer was already well established on Sinai, Athos still hardly knew it because, in that monastery, few were drawn to recollection. Chrysostom counsels all to keep to the simplest forms of mental prayer. Isaac the Syrian[3] says that hardly one out of a thousand people actually practicing mental prayer is capable of attaining to *pure* prayer, the fruit of the great art. It is so partly because the *art* exacts conditions that are

---

[1]The Jesus Prayer.
[2]*Philocalia,* V.
[3]*Isaac the Syrian,* ed. cit., Sermon 16.

not easily come by. On this read Callistus and Ignatius.[4]

The first requisite condition is access to an experienced spiritual director; absolute obedience to him comes next. Then a keen sense of responsibility to God, men, and even things; and the right aim. True humility, a more detailed and sensitive execution of God's commandments, a thorough cleansing of the heart from sins and passions, are all essential. A proud, self-willed decision to acquire through this practice greater spiritual gifts, abilities, or consolations, is a sin and a great danger. And so that the proud and wilful should not come by the method and use it to their own perdition and to the harm of others, the primitive Fathers always alluded to it with great reserve. Pride, the greatest enemy—not of mental prayer only but of all religious practice—lies in wait for us, all along the way.

Therefore John Climacus guardedly says, "May the memory of Jesus blend with your breath; only then will you learn the true value of silence."[5] And Simeon the New Theologian[6] writes of Anthony the Great, "How could he have survived at all, in the dark tomb of heathendom, had he not constantly kept within him the image born of inward prayer?" [388]

I cannot possibly instruct you in the practice of the Jesus Prayer; endless books have been written about it; read them.

But remember that the most important thing of all is humility; then, the ability—not the decision only—always to maintain a keen sense of responsibility towards God, towards one's spiritual director, men, and even things. Remember, too, that Isaac the Syrian warns us that God's

[4]*Philocalia*, V.
[5]*Philocalia*, II.
[6]*Philocalia*, V.

wrath visits all who refuse the bitter cross of agony, the cross of active suffering, and, striving after visions and special graces of prayer, waywardly seek to appropriate the glories of the cross.[7] He also says, "God's grace comes of itself, suddenly, without our seeing it approach. It comes when the place is clean."[8] Therefore, carefully, diligently, constantly clean the place; sweep it with the broom of humility. [342]

Now you are writing sense. Since you say that it is out of a burning desire constantly to implore our Lord for His forgiveness of your dark sins that you long to practice the Jesus Prayer, the whole situation is changed. One well versed in its subtle dangers said, "Only those who always feel like the publican at prayer, and the prodigal son on his way home, can practice it with impunity. Any other who attempts it is pierced with pride of the worst kind. It is good only for the man whose heart sorrows deeply and whose mind is free from worldly chatter; for the mouth that feeds on pig-swill may not feed on the Holy Name."

If you are prepared to persist on this path, get ready for persecution of one kind or another. But be without fear: love and penitence are always at hand for every man's salvation. And you should know that on the way you have now chosen, love begins with awe.

You are, I am sure, aware that for you penitence is now no longer limited to disclosing your sins to your confessor, but that you must now bear your sins in mind always, until your heart nearly breaks with their ugly load; and would break, were it not for your firm faith in the mercy of our Lord.

I pray that my words may give help and not lead you into confusion upon the narrow, thorny path which you now enter. [343: to the same correspondent as 342]

----

[7]*Philocalia,* II.
[8]*Ibid.*

2. Illusions

It is dangerous to assume that our dreams are revelations: this leads to spiritual pride. Ponder calmly: is it likely that a heart and mind, both fully under the influence of all the wildest human passions, can truly mirror divine revelations? Does not such an assumption betray undue reliance on your own *worthiness?* For who can esteem himself worthy of such grace? [268]

You yourself have perfectly described the reason of your woe. First, your education. This, although Christian in theory, did not lead you to a Christian life in practice. Secondly, your early life ran exceptionally smoothly, without any of those temptations and afflictions which—when wrestled with or accepted in the right way—can make true Christians of us. Indeed, when you were a child and when you first grew up, worldlings showered on you much flattery, adulation, and praise. Thus encouraged and helped, unhealthy illusions concerning your importance, superiority, and goodness steadily poisoned your heart, so that even before the cruder passions beset you, pride and a hard self-esteem had built up a sound foundation for your woes.

God resists the proud; He allows them to be humbled by manifold chastisements and by the scorching torments of passion. Your insisting on separation from your first husband was a proof of the hold lusts and passions had gained over you. And, although the situation which naturally ensued could not flatter your pride, it was your pride that had forced the situation.

Then the tentacles of chastisement closed around you! Not only did the fires of a stricken conscience torment you, but, gradually, trifling worries, pin-pricks, annoyances accumulated into a great weight that crushed you, and flattened you out. Still wishing to stamp your will on all around you, you grew agitated and distressed. This agitation and distress, far from acting as a balm to your passions, exasperated them until, at last, your suspicions and jealousy affected your mind.

When your mental balance was once again restored, peace did not return to the home. Far from it. Family quarrels and complications thickened, and now your husband, grown weary, suggests your trying a change, trying to live abroad. *With what judgment ye judge, ye shall be judged: and with what measure ye mete, it shall be measured to you again (Matt. 7:2).*

But do not think, because of all this, that God has forsaken you. No, *for whom the Lord loveth He chasteneth (Heb. 12:6).* Only mind you accept His will humbly, gratefully, peacefully, considering all this, and even greater miseries, nothing but your due. And carefully guard against judging any of those who cause you suffering: they are the weapons of God, working for your betterment and salvation. Remember constantly how far you have drifted from love of God and love of your neighbor. Love of God is manifest in obedience to His commandments; love of our neighbor in love of our enemies. Whosoever is wanting in either of these, is equally far from love of God.

But no matter how little you love God, He still loves you; loves you so much that He showers all this grief and pain on you, making your punishment in this world so great that it may perhaps suffice to amend you, and make unnecessary the dread punishments of the next. These others you may be spared!

Your past and present torments and sufferings are poured down upon you to test your faith and steel it; they also work to curb your lusts and passions. Humble yourself. God succours the humble. Judgment of others, insistence on their shortcomings, can only increase the bitterness of your sorrow. Choose the better part.

Since you ask my advice on your going abroad I must

tell you that I find it unnecessary, and that I fail to see how it can be profitable. Particularly now, after your last talk with your father-in-law. Your husband's parents would clearly prefer you to stay at home; on condition, of course, that you change your behavior, your attitude to things, and your temper of mind. In this I entirely support them. My reasons therefore I have already put before you: your betterment. Staying at home and humbling yourself is the best means thereto. [77]

3. Illusions on Prayer

It is admirable that you should be reading the Fathers. Bear in mind, however, that their writing is like a thick forest: venturing there unprotected, without knowledge and without guidance, we easily go astray and may even run into grave dangers. Many readers have erred from undue self-assurance; whoever attempts a shortcut to the higher life, and sets out wilfully to acquire and appropriate visions and other spiritual joys, calls down on himself the divine wrath.

It is not permitted that we indulge a lust of the mind for the *glories* of the cross. We must not even aspire to them without having first patiently conquered the baser portion of our soul on the way of the Passion, the way to Calvary, the road of supreme agony. Isaac the Syrian says, "Do not imagine that you have left the thicket of passions behind you, until you are well within the walls of the citadel of humility."[9] Read Callistus and Ignatius.[10] Humility, even without works, brings forgiveness. But works without humility are quite useless.

---

[9]*Isaac the Syrian,* ed. cit.
[10]*Philocalia,* V.

Keep to your rule of prayer as rigorously as you would expect any other woman to do, surrounded by her family and living in the world. And see to it, that your prayer is that of the publican, not that of the pharisee.

Keep your conscience keen and bright, and refrain from hankering after, or expecting, consolation. Leave that to God. He knows when, where, and how to give it you. [72]

Once more I must repeat myself: your facile assumption that sensations of bodily warmth, experienced during prayer, are sure signs of special grace, is wrong. They are nothing of the kind, and the assumption that they are is a temptation of the devil. Accept what comes your way with abandonment, and leave it at that, and do not jump to conclusions. [381]

I am astonished, indeed, that not knowing me at all you should choose to describe to me your strange experiences, and ask me to allay your doubts, solve your problems, and give you counsel. Quite frankly, I should much prefer to refuse. Physically weak, sluggish of mind, conscious moreover of having but little insight of soul, how could I find any justification for taking upon me to give advice in such a case as yours?

But I am profoundly touched by your simple faith in direction, and my heart is wrung with compassion for the great dangers you run, the fierce torments you so vividly describe. I have therefore taken counsel with our wisest Fathers and (since God is known to have placed the right word of guidance even in the mouth of dumb beasts) I will try to direct you towards what I take to be the relevant passages in the ancient teaching of our Eastern Fathers, and will strive to warn you against the subtle temptations which lead men like you to think they are glimpsing in visions nothing less than the ineffable truth. By the way, you yourself once mention your suspicions of having strayed into the enemy's nets. Any knowledge of the Fathers would change suspicion to certitude.

According to Gregory of Sinai, this kind of temptation —visions seemingly true but actually false and craftily conjured up by the wily tempter—besets us whenever we strive wilfully to master the great art, before having uprooted pride in the heart's labyrinth, and while our ordinary life is still reeking with sin. God permits this temptation in order that man should come to his senses, do penance and change his ways. But he is left free to do so or not. Realize the full implication of this most important fact: he is left free!

On the strength of your letter, I conclude that the first snare was laid for you in 1853, in the town of T., when you were recovering from a serious illness: you were several times visited by the illusion that as you looked at the icons they changed, until one day rosy rings, detaching themselves from the icon of our Lady, entered your heart bringing with them the firm conviction that you had been granted the pardon of your sins. On the authority of the Fathers, I can assure you that the moment you accepted this as a revelation, and ascribed a moral value to the experience, you fell into the clutches of the devil. All that followed was merely a result of this fall.

Barsanuphius the Great rightly affirms that no devil can conjure forth the form of our Lord; but he says they can easily suggest to the gullible beginner that any kind of form they may have conjured forth actually is our Lord. This must have happened in your apparition of our Lady and Child; but, proud and blind with sin, you failed to see through the trick.

Barsanuphius also tells us that the devil is incapable of evoking the Holy Cross in a man's dreams; and Holy Church proclaims in song: "In Thy Cross, O Lord, hast thou given us a sure weapon; a mighty weapon against our enemy; who shudders, trembles, and creeps away, wounded at the aweful sight."[11] Therefore, your vision of the Metropolitan with Gospels and Cross in hand, and of the host of devils who, clutching your head, made the sign of the cross with it on the floor at his feet, can be nothing but an illusion. The devil fears the Cross but, for your sins and because of your pride, God let him take possession of your fancy, and the devil, while actually showing you some other figure, suggested that it was the Cross. All this he does so as to heighten your confusion.

The same applies to your illusion of devils mockingly repeating after you the words of your prayer. Several of the Fathers make it quite clear that no devil can say the Jesus Prayer which, according to John Climacus, is a potent weapon against them. Therefore, you may be sure that in all such cases, they simply make indistinct noises, and only suggest to you that these are the words of the Prayer. The devils do this in order to prove to you that they fear nothing, which is a lie you must learn to see through. On the whole, the Fathers insist that forms, color, light, singing, and smells—both good and bad—are so many illusions spun by the tempter.

The second snare was laid for you when, wearied by the devil's conjuring tricks, and jogging along a tedious road in your barouche, you gloomily pondered the evil of your life and longed for reconciliation with all whom you had injured and all who were proving hostile towards you. Suddenly you felt a stream of sweet joy flow into your breast. Inexperienced as you are, you assumed this also to be true, not an illusion. Soon you were so entangled in this kind of temptation that you came to the very brink

---

[11]A troparion to the Holy Cross sung in monastery refectories after the evening meal, while the priest-monk on duty stands, crucifix in hand, in the middle of the room, and the monks file past him to kiss it.

of madness. I think God, in His great mercy, prevented your reason from completely foundering only because you had strayed not wilfully, but from lack of experience.

In the seventh Rung, John Climacus says, "Reject with your right hand, the hand of humility, all streams of joy. Lest, since you are unworthy, this joy prove a temptation, and lead you to mistake the wolf for the shepherd." You are constantly mistaking the one for the other. You do so even in the case which you confidently take to be a real experience: when, meditating a text, you felt a blow on your shoulder succeeded by waves of joy that completely engulfed you.

The Apostle says that real spiritual joy is one of the rarest fruits of the spirit, to be attained only near the summit of the way, after all evil habits and thoughts are overcome, all passions conquered, and reconciliation with God is reached. Hence, in your actual condition, you cannot possibly assume that any streams of joy that flow into you or submerge you, no matter how sweet, come from heaven or that you are already partly living there. On this read John Climacus, Rung 15.

As you advance in prayer and spiritual reading, the tempter incessantly warring against you invents more subtle forms of guile. You say that, lately, you often sense the presence of our Lord in your room; then, filled with a joyous tremor, you must fall on the ground at His feet. Your descriptions show that you imagine you see Him as a physical form, physically present in your room: a most dangerous illusion! So are those which you describe as the presence of your guardian angel and of this or that saint, and all you say of your intercourse with them. St. Paul says that Satan can fashion himself into an Angel of Light. Satan does this in order to confuse and confound the inexperienced, and the Fathers are emphatic in guarding beginners against placing any faith at all in such illusions. It is particularly dangerous for you. Read Gregory of Sinai, Chapter 7.

You also say that with the eye of faith you can now see our Lord sitting on the right hand of the Father. Do not indulge this illusion either. The vision of this glory can only be bestowed on those who have conquered all passions and have attained to purity of heart. John Climacus writes, "Do not strive after sight before your hour for seeing has come; but let it approach unbidden, attracted by the goodness of your humility. Then will it blend with you in all purity, for ever and ever."

Describing the first form of the Jesus Prayer, Simeon the New Theologian unequivocally states that untrue visions lead man into the devil's clutches. And Isaac the Syrian, describing the second form, writes, "God's grace comes of itself without any ambitious striving on our part. It will only come to the heart that is pure." And, "should the apple of thine eye be unclean, dare not to raise it; attempt not to gaze at the ball of the sun; lest thy temerity deprive thee even of the limited sight, acquired through simple faith, humility, penance, and other lowly acts and works; lest thy temerity be punished and thou fall headlong into the outer darkness."

It was a mistake for you to practice mental prayer and prayer of the heart.[12] All this is beyond your strength, outside the scope of your capacities, incompatible with your circumstances. Such practices exact the strictest purity of intention towards God, men, and even things. Besides—as Simeon the New Theologian writes on the third form of the Prayer—it should never be undertaken without guidance. Gregory of Sinai[13] describes the spiritual calamities that await those who rashly tread the sacred path. Another point

---

[12]Advanced forms of the Jesus Prayer.
[13]*Philocalia,* V.

of the utmost importance is that you have lately been tossed and harassed by sexual lusts. This always happens when our practices of the Prayer are beyond our abilities and capacities. Read, in the foreword to Philotheus of Sinai,[14] how easily the sensation of heat, caused by prayer, can turn to sexual lust, setting the blind heart on fire, filling the mind with the smoke of lascivious images and thoughts, and causing flesh to yearn for the touch of flesh.

Because of all this, I strongly advise you to stop all practice of the Jesus Prayer. Instead, read or recite—under the direction of your confessor—psalms, penitential canons, litanies and so on. Go to church as frequently as possible; live humbly, according to the admonitions of your conscience; and carefully, according to the commandments of our Lord. In other words, lead the life of an ordinary, God-fearing member of the Christian laity.

You also write that you have long ago given up eating meat. Since, in your case, this is one more occasion for pride, it is not good. Read, in the life of John Climacus, how he always ate, if only a little, of all food permitted by the monastic rule, filing down thereby the horn of self-importance. I advise you to eat meat whenever your family and all God-fearing men do; that is on any day except Wednesdays and Fridays and the days and weeks specially appointed by the Church for fasting. Eat with moderation, of course, gratefully praising our Lord for earth's bounty.

Avoid making idols either of things or of practices.

And it is perfectly absurd to get into debt in order to increase the amount of your charity! Nothing of the kind is mentioned in any book recommended by the Church. In the Old Testament we read: *Every man shall give as he is able, according to the blessing of the Lord thy God*

---

[14]*Philocalia,* III.

which He hath given thee.[15] This, far from encouraging debts, restrains us from rashly giving away anything that our family requires. As to Barsanuphius the Great, he insists that the rich should practice particular discretion in matters of charity, so as not to expose themselves to twofold dangers, moral as well as material.

So far, there is no point at all in our discussing your wish to be a monk. Leave all thought of that until you can think of it seriously: until God shows you that this may be *His* wish. Sometime later, when your children are well established—and if your wife then consents to enter a convent—we can discuss it. But since nuns must keep themselves you will have to provide her with a dowry.

Make a rule never to speak to any one but your confessor either of your illusions or of your temptations.

Now about your having communion every six weeks as you say you have lately been doing. If this is under the direction of your confessor, well and good. But if it is from your own choice, I should advise moderation here too. Limit yourself to twice during each of the three lents of Easter, Sts. Peter and Paul[16] and the Dormition,[17] and once or twice during Christmas Lent.[18] Seven or eight times a year is ample for you at present. This will prevent others' attention centering round you because of your excessive zeal, and will give you less occasion for pride.

It is undoubtedly your duty to teach your family to walk in the fear of the Lord and to instruct them in the ways of a devout life. But it is very wrong of you even to attempt to teach or instruct anyone else. When you try to, you only undermine your own labors. And be particularly careful to avoid all discussions; in these you will

---

[15]Deut. 16:17.
[16]From the eighth day after Pentecost to June 29.
[17]From August 1 to August 15.
[18]From November 15 to December 25.

benefit no one, but may easily do yourself an injury. Try to keep in all things that perfect measure which is the sign of sanctity.

At the end of your letter you say that now, having abandoned the whole of yourself—will, thoughts, heart, soul, body—to God, you are filled with an inexpressible feeling of compassion towards all. But much of your letter flatly contradicts this. In one place you mention how troubled you are by hatred of one or the other person: in another, how sternly you treat your subordinates, and what a fury possesses you when you admonish them: you even say that such people cannot be otherwise treated. All of which not only contradicts your statement but is incompatible with the spirit of the Gospels: for although it is right to admonish those who do wrong, a Christian should do so with the greatest gentleness. As to fury overpowering you, this simply could not be if you were abandoned—body, soul, heart, and will—to God. In other words, your abandonment is nothing but another form of the same illusion which incites you to refrain from eating meat, to give in charity more than you can afford, to communicate more often than other parishioners and the rest of your family, and to attempt forms of prayer that are beyond you.

Callistus and Ignatius write, "Many paths may lead either to salvation or perdition. But one there is which securely leads us heavenward: a life lived according to our Lord's commandments";[19] and so, constantly practice humility, love, and charity, without which none can see God. Nilus of Sora teaches us that the true practice of charity amounts to accepting sorrows, injustice, and persecution. "This—the charity of the spirit—stands as high above bodily charity as soul is raised above flesh."

You, I see, mistakenly assume that evil cannot parade

---

[19]*Philocalia,* V.

under the disguise of impulses which are seemingly good. But Isaac the Syrian writes in Chapter 33, "A desire, to all appearances good, comes from the devil, not from God, whenever it does not tally with a man's unalterable circumstances—outer and inward; it can therefore lead to no good, no matter how much effort he wastes on it."

When the devil suggests that a man should strive after something that is seemingly—but only seemingly—good, it is always unattainable, the devil's object being to lure man into spending himself in pursuit of illusions so that, while missing his real goal, he should live in agony of heart and in great commotion of soul; and all for an illusion, for nothing. Sometimes, the devil may even use seemingly good intentions to spin a web of most harmful temptations. Gregory of Sinai[20] and John Climacus both mention this, and the latter remarks that wilful men are in this way often led to ignore the guidance of experienced directors who could have saved them from folly and despair.[21] Other Fathers stress the extreme difficulty of finding the way between the danger of prematurely aiming too high—or striving after a seeming good—and despondently aiming too low, refraining even from ordinary standards of the Christian life, the life of righteousness. Both temptations, equally dangerous, are snares devised by the devil's guile.

I should like to add that Isaac the Syrian insists on penitence, necessary alike for those who are conscious of sinning greatly and for those who are not; there is no perfection in any of us here on earth. The true signs of sincere penitence are the taming of the beast of anger, and the abstinence from all condemnation of others. Anger is always a sign of great pride. Our Lord calls him who condemns others, oblivious of his own faults, a hypocrite.

---

[20]*Philocalia,* **V, ch.** 7.

[21]*Philocalia,* **II, Rung** 26.

But patience, self-condemnation, and humility guard us against a multitude of temptations and vices.

Do not be angered by my conclusions: although I can perceive in you a sincere desire to come nearer God, I cannot fail to see clearly how sick your soul is. The best medicine for pride, man's greatest sickness of soul, is humility. Words cannot describe or explain it, but the Fathers say that he who strives hard to live according to the precepts of our Lord, and is fully aware of his own sins, acquires it steadily. Therefore be very careful never to think yourself good, or the least bit better than others. [445]

You write that, notwithstanding your joy at hearing from me, my letter made you sad for days. This sadness, the devil's work on the whole, is partly due to your assuming that you had attained to something really worthwhile, whereas you had not: and now, as you put it, perceiving your revolting nakedness you are distressed. To some this sadness might seem good but it is, in reality, a manifestation in you of the Old Adam, the man who, having sinned, could not bear the thought of his nakedness. And yet, is not a man better naked than clothed in filth?

I, for my part, praise the Lord that He should have helped you so completely to accept my advice, based entirely on the teaching of the Fathers. In your circumstances, this gives me great hope that you may soon overcome the host of your illusions.

You ask about the special symptoms of vainglory and pride, and say you can see neither vice in yourself. This is very important, since the very fact that you do not see them proves the grip they have on you: they have formed blind spots in your mind's eye. In spiritual matters, all that is not illumined by the fair light of humility is obliterated by the dark fumes of pride.

Vainglory and pride are very like each other. But vainglory incites us to show off our piety or intelligence and to put much store by the opinion others hold of us; it makes us love praise and go out of our way to get it, and fills us with false shame; whereas pride is chiefly manifested through anger and embarrassment, through the despising, condemnation, and humiliation of others, and through holding oneself—one's own actions and achievements—in high esteem. Pride has made great men—men spiritually great—fall very low. All human misfortunes and all un-Christian actions spring from pride; all good comes from humility.

Refrain from seeking out new ways of prayer in the *Philocalia*: beware lest you fall into new snares from which it may be even more difficult to extricate yourself. Strive after greater simplicity in all things, and seek humility above all else. Pray chiefly that the Lord may help you not to stray from doing His will and that, by means which He alone can know and use, He should show you the right way, and help you to keep it.

You say the enemy still teases you, causing strange noises above your left ear and worrying you in many other ways. This, too, points to your pride; it is, alas, still very strong in you. Therefore I repeat, concentrate on humility. The humble heart conquers enemies, unconquerable to all else. Read Isaac the Syrian, Chapter 72.
[446: to the same correspondent as 445]

You write that you are now profoundly distressed whenever you think of your past life, and that you weep a lot.

It is good that you weep; true penitence requires much weeping. But be careful not to assume that your tears, which spring from a disturbance of your passions, are a grace. John Climacus writes in the seventh Rung, "Mind you do not assume that your tears come from the source of light. This can be true only of him whose passions have been swept away." He also teaches us that tears can have many sources: wrong sorrowing, unquenched vainglory, exasperated lusts and so forth, and that all such tears have little in common with those pure and cleansing tears which wash away sin. He shows too how clever the enemy is in feeding pride on everything; even on the usual signs of humility.

You describe how bitterly you regret the inefficacy of your prayers. Beware: to wish for consolation or revelation in prayer is a sure sign of pride. Pray humbly, in perfect simplicity, seeking salvation only through forgiveness, and having faith that God will extend to you His mercy—as He did to the publican.

Do not juggle with the words of Scripture, stretching them to mean what you want them to. *Shall the thing formed say to him that formed it, Why hast thou made me thus? (Rom. 9:20)* is in no way applicable to your case. According to John Chrysostom these words only affirm that Christians must not grumble about the outer circumstances of their lives, and must realize that on the Day of Judgment all will answer, as equals, for their misdeeds. There is no occasion to think that God, although He has of course permitted your weaknesses, chose them for you or appointed them. On the contrary, He alone can help you to overcome them; He, who unfailingly helps the humble who repent and are grown acutely conscious of their sins.

As the outcome of a sustained desire and impulse you are now using a prayer of your own, which does not entirely correspond either to your inner make-up or to your circumstances: you pray that you may become truly dead unto the world. But such a prayer is only suitable for religious! *You* cannot "die unto the world," simply because of your obligations towards it. Unless you can adjust and adapt your own prayers to your circumstances, you should leave them altogether, and keep to prayers of saintly men. Repeat frequently: Thy will be done, O Lord!

The answer to your question, "How can the enemy call forth heavenly odors in a holy shrine?" is that this is sometimes allowed because of a man's vainglory, self-esteem, and pride. Since such a man seeks consolation, signs of grace and high spiritual gifts, instead of humbly and penitently begging forgiveness and mercy, arch-temptations are allowed to come and torment him.

I perceive that you must be reading the *Philocalia;* but the whole of it is by no means suitable reading for you. Though you may read any of the Fathers on the active life, limit yourself, at present, to John Damascene, John Cassian, and Mark the Ascetic, on spiritual works and the spiritual law. Leave the rest until, with God's help, you shall have overcome your passions; until, living according to the commandments, you shall have acquired the grace of humility.

Isaac the Syrian says that whoever dares to approach the path of mental prayer before he is practiced in the active path, will be visited by God's wrath for seeking sweetness out of season;[22] from which calamity may the dear Lord preserve us! [447: to the same correspondent as 445 and 446]

---

[22]*Philocalia,* II.